REBBE
NACHMAN
AND
YOU

REBBE NACHMAN AND YOU

HOW THE WISDOM OF REBBE NACHMAN OF BRESLOV CAN CHANGE YOUR LIFE

BY

CHAIM KRAMER

Published by
Breslov Research Institute
Jerusalem/NY

First edition

For further information:
Breslov Research Institute, POB 5370, Jerusalem, Israel
or:
Breslov Research Institute, POB 587, Monsey, NY 10952-0587,
USA

Printed in Israel

לזכות

דוד בן חיה עליזה

לזיווג הגון

והצלחה רבה מאוד מאוד

בכל העניינים

זכרון נצח
לעילוי נשמות

הר"ר אברהם ב"ר נפתלי הערץ ז"ל
נלב"ע כ' אלול תשט"ו

*

הר"ר אליהו חיים ב"ר קלונימוס קלמן ז"ל
נלב"ע כ' כסליו תשד"ם

*

הר"ר צבי אריה בן-ציון ב"ר ישראל אבא ז"ל
נלב"ע י"א כסליו תשל"ט

*

הר"ר יחיאל מיכל ב"ר יהושע דוד ז"ל
נלב"ע ה' אב תשס"ו

*

הר"ר קלונימוס קלמן ב"ר אליהו חיים ז"ל
נלב"ע כ"ה טבת תשנ"ט

בעבור שאחד מתלמידם נדב סכום הגון
להדפסת הספר הקדוש הזה לעילוי נשמתם

זכרון נצח
לעילוי נשמות

האשה מזל ב"ר יוסף ע"ה גולדמן
נלב"ע כ"ב תמוז תשנ"ט

*

הרב שמואל מאיר ב"ר צבי אריה ז"ל סלומון
נלב"ע כ"ו אדר תשס"ד

*

האשה יענטה מחלה ב"ר אברהם ז"ל סלומון
נלב"ע ב' חשוון תשנ"ג

*

הילד טוביה ז"ל בן הרב נחמן הי"ו גולדמן
נלב"ע כ"ב תשרי תשס"ח

בעבור שאחד ממשפחתם נדב סכום הגון
להדפסת הספר הקדוש הזה לעילוי נשמתם

TABLE OF CONTENTS

INTRODUCTION

WE'VE NEVER SEEN anything like it in the Jewish world. Rebbe Nachman of Breslov left no successor to his Chassidic movement, yet two centuries after his passing, more and more people are becoming his followers! They come from all sectors of humanity—from the seeker to the indifferent, from the complacent to the antagonistic, from the observant to the atheist—and from all over the globe—from North and South America, Europe, Africa, Australia and Asia.

To where do they come? To Uman, a small city in the Ukraine that still resembles a 19th-century town with its rundown houses and rationed food, water and gas for nearly 90,000 residents. The grave of Rebbe Nachman, located near the old market section, is the site of the annual Breslov Rosh HaShanah *kibutz* (Jewish New Year gathering). Here tens of thousands of people study Rebbe Nachman's teachings and try their best to connect with God through Torah study, prayer, and just "being there" with all those who are seeking a similar spiritual experience.

And what an experience it is!

In 2012 some 30,000 people danced, sang and prayed, twenty-four hours a day, in the synagogues and streets surrounding Rebbe Nachman's grave. The energy was electric, the joy unsurpassed, as each participant soaked up enough spiritual energy to last the rest of the year.

What is it that causes this outpouring of spiritual energy to come to a head in such a faraway and backward locale? What power brings people to leave family and friends and abandon the comforts of home? What is it about Rebbe Nachman and his teachings that invokes such dedication and devotion on the part of his followers to spend Rosh HaShanah with him in minus-one-star accommodations?

And perhaps a more powerful question: Why has Rebbe Nachman become a household word? After World War II, there were maybe 150 Breslover Chassidim worldwide—about ninety in Israel, ten in North America, and maybe fifty who survived the concentration camps and the Soviet NKVD purges of Jews and Judaism. In the 1950s, when I drew close to Breslov, there were very few people in North America who had even heard of Rebbe Nachman or his teachings. Even in the 1960s there were maybe a few hundred Chassidim around the globe. Who are all these people who now come to Uman?

This book was written to address the modern-day phenomenon that is Rebbe Nachman. Who is Rebbe Nachman? What is it about his teachings that excites and motivates people to ask for more? How can a 19th-century Chassidic master from a small town in the Ukraine have so much impact on people in the 21st century? Where is Uman and what is the significance of the pilgrimage to Rebbe Nachman's grave? And are Rebbe Nachman's teachings so relevant that I, too, can benefit from them in the here and now? This book is your introduction to Rebbe Nachman and the Breslover Chassidim. It explains how the movement spread to become the powerful force it is today, with historical data on Reb Noson, the Rebbe's closest disciple. Most importantly, it explains many of Rebbe Nachman's teachings and ideas and their practical relevance in today's world. This is because Chassidut is not just a path in life—it is the way to live a *fulfilled* life, no matter where you live and no matter what you do.

Rebbe Nachman's genius lay in his ability to show future generations the way to live life to the fullest, giving people the tools to do it for themselves. The Rebbe fills our "tool bag" with such basic concepts as joy, simplicity and faith; explains how we can use the tried-and-true tools of Judaism—Torah, prayer and *mitzvot*; outlines the strengths and weaknesses each person has at his or her disposal; and describes the challenges that we face on a daily basis. The Rebbe also speaks often of the Tzaddik—the spiritually moral individual who can illumine the path for many others.

Our Sages teach, "Open up to Me an opening like the eye of a needle, and I will open up for you openings through which oxen and carts can enter!" (*Shir HaShirim Rabbah* 5:3). This book opens up a whole new approach to life in the 21st century, infusing us with the hope that we *can* overcome the obstacles that stand between us and the life we really want to lead. With Rebbe Nachman as our guide, let's discover the path to physical, emotional, spiritual and financial success.

• • •

Our deepest appreciation to Dr. Jay and Paula Novetsky and to Gedaliah and Elisheva Fenster for their generous support in bringing this publication to press. We also thank our editor, Y. Hall, and typesetter, R. Aber, for making this a very readable book.

Chaim Kramer

Sivan 5753/May 2013

LET'S
GET
ACQUAINTED

REBBE NACHMAN AND his main disciple, Reb Noson, lived at a time of great challenge for the Jewish people. Beginning right after the Partitions of Poland in the 1790s, the Russian Czars began issuing decrees to draft Jewish boys into the Russian army for a period of twenty-five years in an attempt to cut off the next generation from any association with Judaism.

The government also began forcing secular education on schoolchildren, alienating youngsters from their Jewish roots. The Czars formed the cruel boundaries of the infamous Jewish Pale of Settlement, banishing Jews from the rural areas and packing them into the cities, where they lived in extreme poverty, having their livelihoods taken away from them.

These decrees, in turn, set the stage for the communities to withdraw into themselves, setting the learned against the ignorant, the *mitnagdim* (opponents of Chassidim) against the Chassidim, the Chassidim against themselves, and, worst of all, Jew against Jew.

Under those conditions, could a rebbe and leader arise who could face these problems head-on and offer encouragement even in the worst of times? Could there be someone to offer comfort to parents whose children were forcibly removed from their homes, and solutions to spiritual alienation? Challenging the cacophony of atheism, is there a voice that rings out with faith and truth to lead the people to God in the wilderness of the "enlightenment" and heresy?

The answer is, "Yes!" In such a world, there is still hope, there is a ray of light. Let's meet Rebbe Nachman and Reb Noson, and discover how we, too, can learn from them.

1

WHO IS REBBE NACHMAN?

REBBE NACHMAN WAS the great-grandson of Rabbi Yisrael, the Baal Shem Tov (Master of the Good Name), founder of the Jewish revival movement known as Chassidut. Rebbe Nachman's mother, Feiga, was the daughter of the Baal Shem Tov's daughter, Adil. His father, Rabbi Simchah, was the son of Rabbi Nachman Horodenker, one of the Baal Shem Tov's closest disciples.

With Chassidut, the Baal Shem Tov revolutionized Jewish life in 18th-century Europe. Until that time, Jewish life centered around the analytical study of Torah, Talmud and other religious texts. Poor and illiterate Jews who were cut off from this scholarship by the demands of working for a living began to be swayed by breakaway Jewish groups and assimilation. The Baal Shem Tov recast the service of God from a scholarly to an emotional and even mystical experience. Through everyday parables masking deep Kabbalistic concepts, he made Judaism something everyone could understand and appreciate. He restored the common man's self-worth by emphasizing the joy that God takes in our simple devotions, such as prayer and acts of kindness.

While the Baal Shem Tov inspired his disciples to create their own Chassidic courts, his influence had begun to wane by the time of Rebbe Nachman's birth. It was up to the Baal Shem Tov's great-grandson to re-infuse Chassidut with spirit and fervor, and he did so in a unique way.

Rebbe Nachman was born in 1772, twelve years after the Baal Shem Tov's passing, in the western Ukrainian town of Medzeboz. The Rebbe had two brothers and a sister. During his childhood, many Chassidic masters would come to visit the grave of the Baal Shem Tov in Medzeboz and they would stay in the Rebbe's parents' house. Rebbe Nachman was deeply inspired by these great leaders to become an outstanding Tzaddik and Torah sage himself. He acquired his first disciple on his wedding day in 1785. Subsequently he became known as a mystic, teacher and storyteller, and eventually a well-known Chassidic master in his own right.

After his marriage he moved to the eastern Ukraine, settling in Ossatin. In the early 1790s he moved to nearby Medvedevka, where he began to attract a devoted following. In 1798-1799, at the height of the Napoleonic wars in the Middle East, he made his pilgrimage to the Holy Land. Returning first to Medvedevka, he moved shortly afterwards to Zlatipolia in 1800. Around this time Rabbi Aryeh Leib, the Shpola Zeide, mounted a bitter campaign of opposition to Rebbe Nachman and his "brand" of Chassidut. This forced Rebbe Nachman to move to Breslov in September 1802.

It was right after Rebbe Nachman moved to Breslov that Reb Noson, who lived in nearby Nemirov, became his student. Reb Noson began to record the teachings and conversations that are Rebbe Nachman's legacy to this day.

The Rebbe furthered the goals of the Chassidic movement by translating the esoteric teachings of the Kabbalah into concrete, practical advice that anyone could use to better his or her own life. Rebbe Nachman knew and could cite any verse or teaching from the entire lexicon of Jewish wisdom—the Tanakh, the Mishnah, the Talmud, the *Zohar* and the Kabbalah—to develop his lessons. In addition to his formal teachings, the Rebbe told stories that contained the deepest mysteries of Torah. He said, "I see that my Torah teachings do not reach you; I will begin telling stories." Rebbe Nachman's innovations in delivering Torah discourses via his intricate lessons, as well as the stories that he told, made him a unique figure in the spread of Chassidut.

Though young in years, the Rebbe was wise to the true meaning of life. He spent much of his time immersed in Torah study and went to great lengths to perfect his character traits and his awe of Heaven. Through his devotions, the ways of God became absolutely clear to him at a young age, and he wrote many pages of advice and counsel to help other people develop for themselves a strong and satisfying relationship with God.

Rebbe Nachman lost his wife, the mother of his eight children, to tuberculosis in 1807. He remarried shortly after. In the late summer of 1807 Rebbe Nachman himself contracted tuberculosis, a disease that ravaged his body for three years. Knowing his time to leave this world was imminent, he moved to Uman in the spring of 1810. Throughout that summer he grew very weak. Despite his illness, his hundreds of followers came to be with him for the annual Rosh HaShanah *kibutz*. He gave over his last lesson on that Rosh HaShanah. A couple of weeks later he passed away, on 18 Tishrei 5571 (October 16, 1810), at the age of thirty-eight. He was buried in Uman the following day.

The Rebbe's two sons and two of his daughters died in infancy; he was survived by four daughters. Without sons to succeed him, it was natural that his Chassidut would die out with its leader. But Rebbe Nachman had a secret that ensured the continuation of his teachings and the growth of his following for generations to come. That secret was his main disciple and scribe, Reb Noson. In the next chapter we will meet the man who guaranteed the survival of Breslov Chassidut for hundreds of years, up to and including our present day.

2

WHO IS REB NOSON?

IN JEWISH HISTORY, every great teacher became that way because he had at least one able student who was able to receive and absorb that knowledge and, later on, disseminate it for future use. After all, without students — and more specifically, *the* student — why would he be known as a great teacher?

About nine miles (fifteen kilometers) from Breslov (a full day's journey by horse and wagon in Rebbe Nachman's time) lay the city of Nemirov, home to Reb Noson Sternhartz, a budding young Torah scholar born in 1780. Reb Noson was the son-in-law of Rabbi Dovid Zvi Ohrbach, the foremost *halakhic* authority of the western Ukraine (Kaminetz-Podolia).

Rabbi Ohrbach was a leading opponent of the Chassidic movement, as was Reb Noson's immediate family. Still, Reb Noson was drawn to the teachings of Chassidut. When Rebbe Nachman moved to Breslov in September 1802, Reb Noson traveled there and was deeply impressed by the teachings and sincerity of Rebbe Nachman and his followers. He immediately began to record the Rebbe's teachings. Later Rebbe Nachman himself asked Reb Noson to record his teachings, saying, "We have to be grateful to Reb Noson, for without him, not one page of my teachings would have remained!" (*Tzaddik* #369).

For the next eight years until Rebbe Nachman passed away, despite all the opposition he faced from his family, Reb Noson became a frequent visitor to Breslov and drew ever closer to the Rebbe. He recorded Rebbe Nachman's lessons, conversations and stories, and observed the Rebbe up close, from which he later wrote the biographical information that we have. Also during that time, Rebbe Nachman instructed Reb Noson to begin writing his own original discourses and prayers. Reb Noson proved himself to be a deep thinker, a prolific writer and a caring and sensitive soul.

Eventually Reb Noson's wife and family acknowledged the positive impact that Chassidut was having on him and withdrew their opposition to Breslov Chassidut. Reb Noson's second son, Reb Yitzchak, became one of his father's most avid disciples. For some twenty-three years until Reb Noson's passing, the two carried on a voluminous correspondence, discussing and strengthening each other in Rebbe Nachman's teachings. These letters were later collected and published as *Alim LiTerufah* (Leaves of Healing), available in English from the Breslov Research Institute as *Eternally Yours*.

When Rebbe Nachman passed away in 1810, Reb Noson was perfectly qualified to succeed him. But he preferred to remain the *de facto* leader, publishing all of the Rebbe's works and guiding the Breslover Chassidim to fulfill the Rebbe's directives. He traveled hundreds of miles each year by horse and wagon to visit and encourage Breslover Chassidim living throughout the Ukraine, and wrote many letters strengthening them to keep following Rebbe Nachman's path.

Even without a living rebbe, Breslov Chassidut expanded and grew. This aroused the jealousy of several of Reb Noson's Chassidic contemporaries, who felt that a Chassidic movement must have a living rebbe to guide it. The Breslover Chassidim became the object of terrible opposition and Reb Noson's life was threatened. Though the opposition grudgingly died down to some extent by the end of Reb Noson's life, it continued to percolate among both Chassidic courts and Lithuanian schools until today.

In the spring of 1811 Reb Noson moved to Breslov and established the annual Rosh HaShanah *kibutz* in Uman. By 1830 the hundreds of attendees at the *kibutz* had outgrown all the local synagogues, and Reb Noson began raising money to build a Breslov *kloyz* (synagogue), which was completed in 1834. Reb Noson merited to see the first volume of his own *magnum opus*, the *Likutey Halakhot*, printed in 1843-1844. He became very weak around Rosh HaShanah 1844 and right after Chanukah of that year, on 10 Tevet 5605 (December 20, 1844), he passed away. He is buried in Breslov.

Reb Noson's efforts and iron will carved and shaped Breslov Chassidut as we know it. By remaining completely true to his master's teachings and transmitting them faithfully, he built a movement that connects later generations directly to Rebbe Nachman himself. Reb Noson neither added to or subtracted from the ideas Rebbe Nachman taught, only expanded and expounded on them in his own writings. We can be assured that the ideas we study and find so helpful today are all rooted in Rebbe Nachman's original teachings and advice given over 200 years ago—with a freshness that makes them seem even more relevant today.

3

WHAT IS BRESLOV?

BRESLOV IS THE NAME of the town in the western Ukraine where Rebbe Nachman spent most of the last eight years of his life, and which gave its name to the Chassidic movement that he founded. One can travel to Breslov today and get a good feel for what it was like to live there in the early 1800s. Aside from a few square meters of cracked asphalt and several telephone and electrical wires, the town looks exactly as it did during Rebbe Nachman's lifetime.

Breslov is sometimes transliterated as Bratslav or Braclav; it should not be confused with Bratislava in Czechoslovakia or Breslau in Germany. Breslov is situated on the Bug River midway between Nemirov and Tulchin, in the area previously known as Kaminetz-Podolia.

It was usual for Chassidic groups of Eastern Europe to take their name from the name of the town where their rebbe and leader lived. When Rebbe Nachman first settled in Breslov in 1802, he said that his followers would always be known as Breslover Chassidim. This is the case today, even though Breslov is now a worldwide movement and there are no known Breslover Chassidim in the town of Breslov itself.

Those who study *gematria*, the system of assigning numerical values to Hebrew letters, find that the name *Breslov* suits the Breslov movement to a T. Rebbe Nachman once pointed out that the name *BReSLoV* (ברסלב) has the same letters as the Hebrew words *LeV BaSaR* (לב בסר, or לב בשר—the letters *samekh* [ס] and *sin* [שׂ] are interchangeable). *LeV BaSaR* is the "heart of flesh" every Jew should have, as in the prophecy of Ezekiel: "I will take away your heart of stone and give you a *LeV BaSaR*, a heart of flesh" (Ezekiel 36:26). Indeed, Rebbe Nachman's teachings have the unique power to turn a "heart of stone" into a caring, feeling "heart of flesh."

Additionally, the name *BReSLoV* (ברסלב) has the same numerical value (294) as *NaChMaN BeN FeIGA* (נחמן בן פיגא, Nachman the son of Feiga), Rebbe Nachman's name and matronymic. It's as if the town was waiting for its Rebbe to arrive and, from there, spread light and knowledge to the entire world.

4

WHY UMAN?

WHILE REBBE NACHMAN LIVED and taught in the town of Breslov for eight years, from 1802 to 1810, he chose to spend the last six months of his life in Uman, a small city in the Ukraine, and to be buried in the cemetery there.

Decades earlier, Uman had been the site of several massacres of Jews by the Haidemaks, a band of peasant Cossacks who overran cities, towns and villages across the entire region in their revolt against the Polish nobility. The first massacre in Uman took place in 1749, when many hundreds of Jews were murdered and part of the city was burned. Count Feliks Potacki, the landlord of the city, rebuilt Uman in 1761; he created a world-famous botanical garden known as Sofiefka Park in the north of the city in the 1790s.

In 1768 the peasants staged yet another revolt. Uman is strategically situated in the center of the Ukraine, about halfway between Kiev to the north and Odessa to the south, and is also a midpoint between east and west. In the 18th century it was a fortified and walled city and could have withstood battles for a long time.

Between 25,000 to 30,000 Jews from the surrounding areas fled to Uman in advance of the Haidemak army and secured themselves behind the city walls. But when the Haidemaks arrived, the governor of Uman betrayed the Jews and threw open the gates, resulting in a three-day massacre of well over 20,000 Jews.

Ivan Gunta, the leader of the Haidemaks, then built a canopy outside the synagogue where some 3,000 Jews had found refuge. He said that anyone who left the synagogue and converted to the Russian Orthodox Church would be spared. No Jew left the synagogue and Gunta murdered them all. Only a handful of the remaining Jews survived.

In 1802 Rebbe Nachman passed through Uman on his way to the town of Breslov. Seeing the cemetery and recognizing the sanctity of the Jewish martyrs buried there, Rebbe Nachman remarked, "It would be good to be buried here." In 1810 he chose to return to Uman to be buried among the martyrs.

Reb Noson, who shepherded the expansion of the Breslov movement after the Rebbe's passing, realized that Uman, rather than Breslov, should be the focal point of the Chassidut because the Rebbe was buried there. He invested much time and effort to encourage Chassidim to join the annual Rosh HaShanah pilgrimage to the Rebbe's grave. He also constructed a large synagogue in Uman to accommodate the hundreds of Chassidim who traveled there. In 1866 Reb Noson's main disciple and successor, Reb Nachman of Tulchin, moved to Uman permanently and led the Breslover Chassidim from there.

Besides the annual Rosh HaShanah pilgrimage to Rebbe Nachman's grave, Uman became a magnet for visitors at any time of year. Its popularity is based on a unique promise that the Rebbe made about half a year before he passed away. At that time, Rebbe Nachman revealed the *Tikkun HaKlali* (General Remedy), the Ten Chapters of Psalms one should recite in order to rectify sexual sins. The Rebbe then testified in the presence of two witnesses: "Whoever comes to my grave, recites the Ten Chapters of Psalms and gives something to charity, I will extend myself the length and breadth of Creation for him; by his *peyot* (sidelocks), I will pull him out of Gehinnom!"

No one before or since ever made such a promise. As a result, thousands of people made the effort to travel to Rebbe Nachman's grave in Uman. During the Communist era from 1917 to 1989, travel to Uman was restricted and anyone who was caught there risked being deported to Siberia—or worse. But come they did, and they kept coming—from Israel, England and America, where new Breslover communities were founded after the Holocaust. More and more people pounded on the gates until finally the Iron Curtain crumbled and the way was opened for all.

Today over 30,000 people travel to the annual Rosh HaShanah *kibutz* in Uman. You can find a minyan for prayers there every Shabbat. It's never been easier to travel to Uman and reap the benefits of praying by the Rebbe's grave.

5

HOW DOES REBBE NACHMAN SPEAK TO ME?

AT FIRST GLANCE IT doesn't seem possible. How can the words of a 19th-century Chassidic master from a small town in the Ukraine speak to people living in the 21st-century metropolises of the Western world? What does Rebbe Nachman know of the modern age—its scientific and technological breakthroughs; its advances in medicine, genetic engineering and telecommunications; its phenomena of global interdependence and cyber-terrorism?

If you think that way, you don't know Rebbe Nachman.

Rebbe Nachman lived at a pivotal point in world history. Standing on the verge of the modern age, which would introduce both an industrial revolution that would totally transform the way people lived, and an ideological revolution that would shake the entire framework of beliefs and assumptions on which people had based their lives for centuries, Rebbe Nachman said, "I'll tell you a secret. A great wave of atheism is about to enter the world" (*Rabbi Nachman's Wisdom* #220). One of the Rebbe's main objectives was to throw out spiritual life rafts to those who would become engulfed in the impending ideological torrent.

So many people who read Rebbe Nachman's works have the uncanny feeling that he is talking directly to them. With startling clarity, he pinpoints the real trials of our modern age: the breakdown in personal and familial relationships; the rising incidence of depression, anxiety and other mental disorders; the overdependence on drugs, alcohol and other soul-numbing diversions; the existential loneliness that we feel even as we are surrounded by more wealth and possessions than any generation has ever known. The Rebbe saw clearly that further sophistication is not the answer. "The greatest wisdom of all," he declared, "is to be simple." "*Gevalt!*" he cried. "Don't give up!"

Rebbe Nachman shows us how to navigate the challenges of this world and make a success of our lives. To that end, he presents both the timeless tools of Torah, prayer, *mitzvot* and charity, and his own original teachings on joy, simplicity, faith, looking for the good points, and many others. His teachings about the Tzaddik hold out tantalizing opportunities for us to infuse our lives with more holiness and morality. Throughout his writings, Rebbe Nachman always encourages, never chastises. Even to the person who feels he is so sunk in his sins that he can never rise again, Rebbe Nachman assures, "There is always hope. Every day you have the power to start anew."

Rebbe Nachman speaks to everyone who is searching for answers. Let's hear what he has to say.

BRESLOV
BASICS

JUDAISM HAS ONE ROOT: the Torah. That root has its own Root, which is God. It stands to reason that since the one Torah is from the One God, there should not be variations in it—or at least not too many. Yet even a cursory glance at those who study Torah will find many paths, many interpretations and many approaches. But all Torah teachings are meant to call out, "God is One." What makes one set of teachings more powerful than another?

Rebbe Nachman once said, "I'm leading you on a new path that is really very old" (*Tzaddik* #392). The Rebbe was a very creative thinker who was able to see everything in terms of Godliness and, at the same time, see everything from the vantage point of the human being. Using the standard works of Judaism—the Torah, Mishnah, Talmud, *Shulchan Arukh*, *Zohar* and Kabbalah—as a starting point, the Rebbe charted new paths for modern man to find physical, emotional and spiritual fulfillment in this world.

This section outlines the Rebbe's well-known concepts such as free will, faith and truth, finding joy and peace, and how to effect a *tikkun* (rectification) for the mistakes we've made. He also speaks about the importance of finding the Tzaddik, the leader that we all need—after all, it was Moses who led the Jews out of slavery in Egypt, and King David who forged the Jewish people into a cohesive unit and the leading nation of its time. A leader is a leader, one who actually leads, not follows.

Each topic concludes on a personal note, offering insights and practical tips for incorporating Rebbe Nachman's ideas into our own lives.

6

WHAT IS FREE WILL?

Someone once asked Rebbe Nachman, "What is the idea of free will?"

"Very simple," Rebbe Nachman replied. "If you want, you do it. If you don't want, you don't do it."

Reb Noson adds: "I have recorded this because it is very necessary for people to know. A lot of people are very confused because they have gotten used to their actions and are steeped in their habits for many years, and it seems to them as if they don't have freedom to choose anymore and can no longer control their ways. But the truth is not so. Every person always has freedom to choose in everything. A person acts the way he wants to. Understand this very well" (Likutey Moharan II, 110).

WHAT IS FREE WILL? It is the ability to choose to do whatever you wish to do, whenever you wish to do so, in any kind of situation. Knowing that you have this power, you can take any idea or suggestion that you hear and apply it for your benefit. As Reb Noson explains, free will is the most amazing power in the entire world (*Likutey Halakhot, Birkhot HaShachar* 5:74).

"What's so amazing about it?" you may ask. Well, consider that you are a king, a ruler, or even a democratically elected leader. Of course you want people to follow you and do what you think is best for the land you rule. In that case, would you give anyone, let alone *everyone*, the power to choose to rebel against you?

But that is exactly what God did when He created the world! He entrusted man with *da'at* (intellect) and gave him several commandments to obey—without any spiritual policemen standing over him. We are allowed to do whatever we want! This is the incredible power of free will.

As with all aspects of Creation, the Kabbalah offers us a closer look at how free will came about, and Rebbe Nachman explains from this how we can apply it to our daily lives. The great Kabbalist Rabbi Yitzchak Luria (known as the ARI) describes the way God brought the world into existence:

> Before all things were created...the Supernal Light was complete and perfect. It filled all existence. There was no empty space, since everything was filled with that Light of the Infinite. There was no category of beginning and no category of end.
>
> When it arose in God's Will to create worlds...He withdrew His Infinite Essence from the very center point of His Light. He then withdrew that Light even further, distancing it to the extremities around this center point, leaving a Vacated Space. After this constriction, there was a *place* for all that was to be created. God then drew a single, straight *Kav* (Ray) down from His Infinite Light into the Vacated Space...Through this *Kav*, the Light of God spreads forth and flows down into the universes that are located within that Space (*Etz Chaim, Drush Igulim v'Yosher* 1:2).

We learn from this teaching that God is hidden—He withdrew Himself, as it were, from the Vacated Space—yet He drew a Ray of His Infinite Light *into* the Vacated Space, which He uses to sustain all the universes, all of mankind, and all the other levels of this material world, animal, vegetable and mineral.

The concealment of God is what allows for free will. Were God to be manifest in the Vacated Space, man would have no option as to what to do. Being in God's presence at all times, man would be forced to serve Him. That kind of service would be robotic. But God wanted people to have free choice, to use their intellect to guide themselves and their lives on a path that will be good and productive. Therefore God withdrew Himself, as it were, and the universe in which we live seems devoid of Godliness. We are not robots, nor are we clones—we are thinking individuals with free will to do as we choose.

So, "Go ahead! Use your free will and do whatever you want!" But on the other hand, as we have seen, God drew a Ray from His Infinite Light that sustains all of creation into the Vacated Space. He *is* here, present at all times. So again, "Go ahead! Use your free will, because you *can* seek God and you *can* find Him!"

The Vacated Space—the world as we know it—is a paradox. God is not here, because otherwise we would be forced to serve Him. But God *must* be here, otherwise what sustains the universe? But He cannot be here! But He must be here! But He cannot be here! But He must be here!

This paradox is what gives man free will. God is concealed, yet He created man with a mind and granted him intellect. Man can choose to search for God or neglect Him, or even rebel against Him. God is, of course, here.

As Rebbe Nachman said, "God is always with you. He is near you! He is next to you! Do not be afraid!" (*Siach Sarfey Kodesh* III, #661). But He remains concealed. By searching for Him, we can find Him, for He is always close by, right next to us, actually waiting for us to turn to Him. And when we search, we find: God becomes revealed to us.

But even when God becomes revealed, man still has free will, because in essence, God is still concealed from us. Since God is Infinite, there are layers upon layers of Godliness waiting to be discovered. When a person uses his free will in the direction of searching for God, the layers unfold one by one and he finds himself drawing ever closer to God.

WHAT DOES THIS MEAN TO ME ?

Most people think of themselves as creatures of habit, but Rebbe Nachman tells us that we needn't be slaves to our impulses. We *can* respond differently. We *can* exercise discipline. Rebbe Nachman likens self-control to a rider on a horse that has gone astray. All the rider has to do is grab hold of the reins to return it to the path (*Likutey Moharan* II, 50). As long as we keep life simple, we can maintain control over many facets of our lives.

If I'm unhappy at my job or face problems in my marriage, should I walk out? Did you ever see a baseball team walk off the field in the seventh inning when the score was against them, 13-1? Obviously not. If giving up was our reaction every time we felt despondent, not only would *we* be in hot water, but the entire world would fall apart if everybody acted so irresponsibly. We can't just walk away from every trouble, so do we really have "free" will? The answer is, "Yes!"

Our Sages advised: Every person must say, "The world was created for me" (*Sanhedrin* 37a). What does that mean? It means that every person is important—and especially you. It's true. You come first. The world was created for you. The only thing is, as Rebbe Nachman explains, this privilege carries responsibility. Because the world was created for you, you must see to its rectification. *You* are responsible for the world (*Likutey Moharan* I, 5:1). At any and all times, you can choose to do whatever you want to do. It's just a matter of acting responsibly. It's that simple.

So instead of telling yourself, "I can't," tell yourself, "I can." In a moment, you and I and everyone else can turn our lives around. Or at least begin to turn them around. And when we apply this idea of "I can" to our work, our studies and any of our habits, we'll see that we certainly can control our thoughts, even if only for a few moments. We can seize control of our minds and focus. We can remain steadfast in our resolve.

One of Rebbe Nachman's keen insights is that a person should learn to live in the present. "Today!" (*Likutey Moharan* I, 272). By living in the present, we don't have to suffer the burden of long-term diets or devotions or commitments. All we have to worry about are our efforts for "today." Concentrating for the short term is easier; being responsible for a limited time is bearable.

It's really very simple, though admittedly not so simple after all. Many factors are involved, including how strong is your resolve to choose the right path, and how strong is your ability to follow it through, despite challenges that seem overwhelming. But when you know and understand that it is *your* choice, stemming from your free will, that determines what happens in your life, then you have the solid foundation to face and overcome the vicissitudes of life.

And it's very helpful to remember Rebbe Nachman's statement: "Everything you see in this world, everything that is created, is all for the sake of man's free will" (*Tzaddik* #519).

7

WHAT IS SIMPLICITY?

Before he passed away, Reb Noson was heard sighing very deeply. When asked why he sighed, he replied, "I prayed as best I could, I studied what I felt I could, I performed my other devotions the best I could. I am sighing because I don't know if I fulfilled Rebbe Nachman's directive of simplicity as I should have!" (Oral tradition).

OF ALL OF Rebbe Nachman's major teachings, simplicity is probably the least understood. Yet it has a major impact on the way we live our lives.

Once, when speaking about God, Rebbe Nachman said that God is very complex—but He is really very, very simple (*Rabbi Nachman's Wisdom* #101). As we know from the *Shema*,* God is One, totally unique. In any number more than one, we find complexity. But when we deal with a simple, single unit, there is no duplicity and no conflicts exist. Rebbe Nachman implies that when we learn to simplify our lives, we can experience more serenity and tranquility.

---

* *"Shema Yisrael*—Hear, Israel! God is our Lord. God is One" (Deuteronomy 6:4).

If asked to describe a "simple" person, you might give a negative description, a picture of someone who is dull-witted, foolish or even imbecilic. Saying something is "simple" conjures up the image of commonplace and inconsequential at best. That is not at all what the Rebbe had in mind. Instead, he looks to the Torah's meaning of the word "simple," as our patriarch Jacob is described as a *tam*, a simple man (Genesis 25:27). A *tam* is someone who is unassuming, sincere, straightforward. He lacks guile and shuns twisted reasoning. Simplicity implies wholeness and singularity, suggests freedom from mixture and convolutions, and denotes something pure and unadulterated.

Nowadays, achieving simplicity can be as elusive as defining it. The glitz and glitter of new fads and designer products prevent us from appreciating and cherishing that which is unadulterated. All too often we allow our imagination to dominate our perspective of reality, letting it lead us away from the genuine and the sincere, away from the straightforward and the simple truth.

Simplicity means clarity. "I do one thing at a time. I am not under pressure to be a superman." Every person can focus on the one task that requires his immediate attention and do what is necessary, better and faster than if he were concentrating on several things at once.

Today many psychologists and therapists counsel their clients to keep their lives simple. Instead of living in huge homes that cost a fortune to heat, or purchasing loads of clothes and utensils that clog our closets and are seldom used, they suggest we buy less and use less, saving money, space, the environment and everything else. Why do we need so many cell phones, MP3s, beepers and a whole array of electronic equipment just to keep up with the Goldbergs and the Schwartzes? True, these gadgets make our lives easier, but at what cost?

An important caveat: Simplicity does not mean believing whatever anyone tells you and foolishly falling victim to dishonesty and falsehood. That would be gullibility, not simplicity. Our Sages warned us in this regard: Respect, yet suspect that which is unfamiliar to you (cf. *Derekh Eretz Zuta* 5). Rebbe Nachman specifically warned us to be very careful in financial matters (see *Likutey Moharan* I, 69; cf. *Rabbi Nachman's Wisdom* #281) and to be wary of placing our physical well-being and/or emotional welfare in the hands of "reliable" professionals and "tried and tested" solutions (ibid., #50). While the simple person leaves his mind open, neither forming an immediate opinion nor trying to second-guess the "true" motives of other people, he won't gullibly subscribe to the latest advice, trend, investment or fad that comes his way. Though by taking things at face value, one may well open himself up to dubious and possibly even harmful influences, Reb Noson quotes a proverb of King Solomon: "He that follows the simple path goes securely" (Proverbs 10:9).

The rule is: Accept, but be careful. To paraphrase Rabbi Eliyahu Chaim Rosen, my *Rosh Yeshivah*: "It is a pleasure dealing with people. They are trustworthy, they are honest, they are decent people. But always remember to count your change!"

WHAT DOES THIS MEAN TO ME ?

At the end of his story, "The Exchanged Children" (*Rabbi Nachman's Stories* #11), Rebbe Nachman speaks of a prince who was challenged to figure out the mystery of a certain throne. Close by the throne were animals and birds carved out of wood, a bed, a table, a lamp and a chair. Having the gift of understanding one thing from another, the prince realized that the throne was a symbol of peace—but only if everything was in its proper place. He started moving things around, this item a little bit, that item a little bit, until everything was in its place. Then there emerged from the throne the most beautiful melodies of harmony and sweetness.

This is the path to simplicity: Everything in its place, everything in its own time. Instead of the convoluted, speculative paths that people often choose, try to seek the simplest solution. This way, you avoid inner conflict, for a simple, singular path has no diversity and thus offers little or even nothing to distract you. Then you can remain focused on your goals.

Rebbe Nachman was known for never forcing an issue, as if it had to be done immediately or in a certain way (see *Tzaddik* #430-435). That kind of approach never works (and also turns other people off). The simple approach *will* work. It will never work to try and lose ten pounds in a day, but little by little we can lose a few ounces until we reach our goal. It never works to try to save a lot of money in a very short period of time, but by saving a little at a time—especially with compound interest—we can amass a great deal of money. Like the prince, we should take small, effective steps. The results are harmony within, peace at home and accord with our friends, neighbors and coworkers.

Simplicity also means breaking down goals into manageable bites. For example, a person who wants to study the entire Talmud has chosen an important goal, but it cannot be done in one day. It requires simplifying the task, one page at a time. "That's all I need to do." Cleaning a house for the Pesach holiday nowadays is a humongous task. But it can be accomplished, one room at a time. The same applies to learning new skills, building a relationship, and everything else you aspire to.

As you pursue the simple path, you'll find it influences your ability for positive thinking. "After all, I *can* do this; it's not that complicated or difficult." If I'm not weighed down with the burden of paying an exorbitant mortgage instead of a more moderate one, because I'm not looking for the "best" or the "fanciest" (and the same applies to buying a car, furniture, appliances and so on), then I can breathe easier. I can concentrate. I can focus. I have more time and energy for the important things.

With simplicity, we have the freedom to accomplish far more than we could ever imagine.

8

WHAT IS JOY?

Rebbe Nachman teaches: It is a great mitzvah to be happy always.

Strengthen yourself to push aside all depression and sadness. Everyone has lots of problems and the nature of man is to be attracted to sadness. To escape these difficulties, constantly bring joy into your life—even if you have to resort to silliness (Likutey Moharan II, 24).

YOU'D THINK THAT being told to be happy is superfluous. Who doesn't know this? Is it really necessary to coax, urge and encourage people to be happy? It's a natural desire, not one that has to be worked on. Or is it?

"True joy is the hardest thing of all," Rebbe Nachman insists. "You must *force* yourself to be happy all the time" (*Advice*, Joy 35).

Life certainly gives us enough excuses to be worried. *How* am I going to meet the tuition payment? *What* did you say happened to the car? *Who* did you say you're bringing home for dinner?! And we're not even mentioning health issues. The list is endless. Your alternatives: joy or depression.

Depression, though, is your worst enemy. Rebbe Nachman compares depression to the bite of a serpent (*Likutey Moharan* I, 189). Just as a serpent strikes suddenly, so does depression. All of a sudden it hits and you're left wondering how you can ever be happy again. My *Rosh Yeshivah*, Rabbi Eliyahu Chaim Rosen, used to say, "People think that difficulties are unexpected in life. They're surprised when troubles attack and sadness comes. But even if a person were to live for a thousand years, he would still have a long list of problems waiting for him. When one leaves, another is sure to follow on its heels. This is an axiom of life."

It's a cycle. Something unexpected happens and we get annoyed. The doldrums and depression, still mild, are on the horizon. We're already less tolerant of whatever happens next. Naturally, we anticipate everything going wrong. And it does! At the same time, we get angry, experience greater failure, become more depressed, and feel more discouraged and lethargic. The serpent of sadness has struck and its poisonous venom of depression begins to spread without our being aware of what actually happened.

Interestingly enough, depression, sadness and suffering are necessary ingredients in the world. Our Sages state, "Whoever mourns Jerusalem will yet share in its rejoicing" (*Ta'anit* 30b). Without experiencing sorrow and mourning, there is no way for us to appreciate its opposite. We have nothing with which to compare our happiness. Therefore we experience suffering. Only then can we know the true taste of joy. And because some sadness and suffering is necessary, Rebbe Nachman urges us to strive for joy. We have to use all our strength to attain happiness, since only by being happy will we have the necessary faith, courage and strength to face our sorrows and burdens and overcome them.

WHAT DOES THIS MEAN TO ME ?

Joy puts you on the fast track to achieving any goal you desire. Therefore Rebbe Nachman emphasizes the importance of being joyous at all times. While it's easy to be happy when you feel good and things are going smoothly, what should you do when you don't feel happy and there's nothing to be joyous about? Rebbe Nachman offers these suggestions for getting back on track:

FORCE YOURSELF. The importance of joy is so great that you should make every effort to be happy. This can be compared to a group of people who are dancing in a circle while a sad person looks on. They reach out and pull him in to join them, whereupon he leaves his depression off to the side. However, when the newcomer stops dancing, his depression returns. Though the few minutes of joy are valuable, still, it would be better to bring the depression itself into the circle of happiness and keep it there (*Likutey Moharan* II, 23). Forcing yourself to be happy will eventually turn the cause of your unhappiness into a real source of joy.

Someone once asked Reb Noson how he could be happy when he had so many problems and difficulties. Reb Noson answered, "Borrow the happiness!" (*Siach Sarfey Kodesh* 1-736). When it comes to money, we rarely hesitate to borrow against future earnings. Well, sadness makes a person feel he's missing something. The thing to do, as Reb Noson advises, is to borrow from whatever you can think of that makes you happy. Besides, there's a big difference between owing money and owing happiness. When money is paid back, it hurts a little. But with happiness, when we pay it back, we have happiness again. Forcing joy and happiness actually pays fantastic dividends!

FAKE IT. Even if you don't feel happy, you can fake it. Pretend to be happy. Who says that if you're feeling down, you can't smile? We fake a smile often enough when trying to be polite; why not now? Try it. A smile, even a pasted-on grin, is contagious. Not only will it make others happy when they return your smile, but as studies show, smiling relieves tension and really does make your outlook on life a lot brighter (cf. *Rabbi Nachman's Wisdom* #43).

REMEMBER YOUR GOOD POINTS. Another way you can become joyous when depressed is by acknowledging that you have at least some good within you. Even if you can't find anything good in yourself, you still have what to be happy about: "I am a Jew!" (*Likutey Moharan* II, 10). Simply be happy that you can feel proud and joyous about your heritage, which is not even your own doing, but a gift from God (more about this in Chapter 11, "What are the Good Points?").

SING, PLAY MUSIC AND DANCE. Music clears the mind and makes us happy. Music has the power to help us pour out our heart before God. It also has the power to sharpen our memories and enable us to concentrate on our goals (*Advice*, Joy 14-15). Therefore Rebbe Nachman says it's a very good habit to inspire ourselves with a melody. The spiritual roots of music and song are quite exalted and can arouse our hearts and raise our spirits (*Rabbi Nachman's Wisdom* #273).

The Rebbe also talks about the special power that dancing and clapping have to make us happy and mitigate the negative things affecting us (*Likutey Moharan* I, 169). It is customary in every Breslov synagogue to dance each day after the morning and evening prayers. Many Breslover Chassidim dance after learning together, and some even dance daily by themselves. It's a sure-fire way to arouse feelings of joy and happiness.

DO SOMETHING SILLY. In talking about making every effort to be joyous, Rebbe Nachman said this even includes resorting to acting a bit silly. The price one pays for a little silliness is far less than the price of depression and lethargy.

Echoing the message found in Chapter 6 about free will: There is joy, there is depression. Which path do I choose? Rebbe Nachman says it depends on how you view yourself. If you look for the good, then you think good, things are positive and you can be joyous. The opposite is also true. So choose happiness.

Reb Avraham Chazan commented, "If Rebbe Nachman taught that it's a great mitzvah to be happy always, then we must believe that there is what to be happy about!" (*Rabbi Eliyahu Chaim Rosen*).

9

WHAT IS PEACE?

There is peace that lacks a mouth. And there is a peace that has a mouth (Likutey Moharan I, 57:8).

PEACE IS ONE OF those things that everyone wishes for and few people actually experience. We all want world peace, peace in the Middle East, peace on the home front and peace between brothers. Everyone wants a peaceful life. Who needs aggravation, enmity, deceit or underhanded dealings? But invariably, life is more about war than peace. Why do strife and conflict flare up so quickly?

Rebbe Nachman explains that it all starts with the individual. If we lack inner peace, the whole world becomes fragmented. If we possess inner peace, then tranquility and harmony spread throughout the world.

How does this work? The Rebbe explains that all strife is identical. We may think that our neighbors aren't talking to each other because one slighted the other, or that two nations are squabbling over a piece of land, but in reality all strife stems from people's different and/or opposing traits. As Rebbe Nachman puts it:

The friction within a family is a counterpart of the wars between nations. Each person in a household is the counterpart of a world power, and their quarrels are the wars between those powers. The traits of each nation are also reflected in these individuals. Some nations are known for anger, others for bloodthirstiness. Each one has its particular trait. The counterparts of these traits are found in each household.

You may wish to live in peace. You have no desire for strife. Still, you are forced into dispute and conflict. Nations are the same. A nation may desire peace and make many concessions to achieve it. But no matter how much it tries to remain neutral, it can still be caught up in war. Two opposing sides can demand its allegiance until it is drawn into war against its will. The same is true in a household.

This is because man is a miniature world (*Zohar* III, 33b; *Tikkuney Zohar* #69, 100b). His essence contains the world and everything in it. A man and his family contain the nations of the world, including all their battles (*Rabbi Nachman's Wisdom* #77).

It's even worse for a person who lives alone. Rebbe Nachman says that a man living in isolation can go insane from the effect of all the warring nations within him. While someone who lives among family and friends can express the nation's battles through his interactions with other people, the man who lives alone must play the role of all the nations. Each time a nation is victorious, he must change his personality, which can drive him insane.

Now we understand why war is the norm. Our different personalities naturally lead to conflict, and that creates friction both among the people we live with and people we've never met. However, if man is a microcosm of the world, the reverse should also be true. And it is. If each of us could attain inner peace, we could bring peace to the world at large!

• • •

REBBE NACHMAN FURTHER teaches that there are two kinds of peace. "Peace that lacks a mouth" is a cease-fire. It's peaceful, it's quiet, there's no active shooting off of the guns (or the mouth) and attacking people. But it's not a very comfortable situation. People who aren't engaged in active combat may still harbor some pretty nasty feelings about each other, and lack of communication can lead to serious breaches of the peace. The optimal kind of peace is "peace that has a mouth." Dialogue takes place, compromises are reached, nations join together, and people even celebrate with each other.

The Hebrew word for peace, *ShaLoM* (שלום), comes from the same root as the word *SheLeiMut* (שלמות), "completeness" or "perfection." Peace implies a unity, where everyone or everything is together as one. When we are focused on unity, we can be as dissimilar as we want, because we are at peace (see *Likutey Halakhot, Prikah u'Te'inah* 4:23).

WHAT DOES THIS MEAN TO ME ?

Inner peace is a truly remarkable achievement. The person who is comfortable with himself and feels at ease with whatever situation he finds himself in can accomplish tremendous things during his life. Just examine the fellow who is comfortable with himself: he exudes self-confidence, is a pillar of strength, and emerges as a sea of tranquility amid all the tumult around him. Because he is willing to avoid combative situations, even when it might seem to be to his detriment, he emerges from every fracas unscathed. As he radiates that inner peace outwards, influencing those around him, eventually he can spread peace far and wide.

How we can acquire inner peace for ourselves?

The Talmud relates that Rabban Gamliel once saw a ship go down at sea with its travelers, among them Rabbi Akiva. A short while later Rabbi Akiva came before Rabban Gamliel, who was very surprised to see him. Rabban Gamliel asked, "How did you survive?" Rabbi Akiva replied, "I found a block of wood and held on tightly. And for each wave that swept over me, I simply bowed my head."

My *Rosh Yeshiva*, Rabbi Eliyahu Chaim Rosen, often told this story and explained that a block of wood represents silence. We are in the sea of life and floundering because of all the waves that overwhelm us. The trick to survival is to act like a block of wood that is silent—it cannot reply to any insult or demeaning comment. Additionally, we must learn to "bow our heads" before each wave—this helps us duck below the radar of wars and unwelcome situations. Then, when the wave passes—as it always does—we can pick up our heads and go forward.

This is a most wonderful piece of advice on how to attain inner peace. When we face a combative situation head-on, usually we are standing in harm's way. But if we "roll with the punches" and avoid getting into arguments, we can emerge unscathed or with a minimal amount of damage.

Rebbe Nachman adds that certain Jewish practices are especially helpful for attaining inner peace and promoting peace in the world. They are:

- Giving charity
- Studying *halakhah* (the Jewish legal codes)
- Safeguarding one's moral purity
- Increasing one's fear of Heaven

The highest peace is the peace between opposites. You know the kind of person we're talking about—he just has to look your way and your skin starts crawling. The next time you meet someone who makes you uncomfortable, try to think of ways for the two of you to get along. You'll be doing a huge service both for your own, inner peace and for the world peace we all long for. When you overlook other people's shortcomings and look for the good in them, you will be at peace with everyone.

10

WHAT IS SUFFERING?

When asked how things are, a person should reply that they are going well, thanking God for his situation even if things are actually very difficult. If he does this, then God says, "This is what you call good? I'll show you what good really is!" (Siach Sarfey Kodesh 1-32).

SOMETIMES LIFE SEEMS to be little more than an endless stream of problems to solve and obstacles to overcome. Whether our difficulties are personal, communal or national, there seems to be no escaping them. Occasionally their sheer number or weight causes a person to lose faith. Why does God send difficulties our way?

Many philosophers have pondered the conundrum: How can a loving God inflict suffering on His creatures? Or as more than one contemporary observer has phrased it, "Why do bad things happen to good people?"

In Jewish thought, difficulties and misfortune are not "bad" or punishments, but challenges. Challenges are the primary vehicle for testing our mettle and seeing what we're really made of. In the field of health and exercise, everyone knows, "No pain, no gain." If you don't sweat a little when you work out, pushing yourself a little bit further than you did yesterday, you'll never get fit. Similarly, if God wouldn't put us in difficult situations—or even oppressive and crushing situations—we would never build our spiritual muscles and find out what we're capable of achieving.

Difficulties also force a person to cry out for relief—which is exactly what God is waiting for. God wants a personal relationship with each one of us, and the relationship can't be just one-way, with God giving and giving and us taking and taking. When God gives us something to cry about and we cry out to Him, we take our relationship to the next level.

How can we be sure that it's really God Who's behind our difficulties? It sure seems like it's that obnoxious downstairs neighbor who keeps us up all night with his raucous music, or that conniving coworker who keeps reporting our every misstep to the boss in the hope of getting us fired and him promoted. Where is God in the equation?

A young man once came to me bemoaning his life. He was born somewhere in Kansas and had a standard, non-Jewish education in public schools. At twenty-five, he discovered his Jewish roots. "What happened to the twenty-five years of my life that I lost?" he demanded. I asked him, "Who put your soul in Kansas?! It was God Who placed you there, knowing beforehand how you'd grow up. Your life begins when you are cognizant of God and that He is the Master Chess Player moving us, the pieces, around the board." The same is true for all of us. When we are ready to accept that God is behind the bad times as well as the good, then we can actually see our life experiences falling into an amazing pattern, making us aware that there is Somebody behind all the problems (and successes) in our lives.

Rebbe Nachman adds an intriguing observation: Even in the midst of the worst misfortune, we can see evidence of God's kindness! (*Likutey Moharan* I, 195). In every distress, God offers us some measure of relief. For a dialysis patient who must come three times a week to the hospital for hours-long treatments, it may be a nurse who goes out of her way to make sure he has a comfortable pillow and his favorite reading material by his side. For many a grieving child, there is the knowledge that "we did what we could" and that his parent's suffering wasn't an extended battle for endless years, or that the pain was minimal. And even if things are very, very difficult, we know that they could always be worse. That thought alone provides great consolation.

Reb Noson suffered terrible opposition during the years 1834 to 1838 when he served as the de facto leader of the Breslover Chassidim after Rebbe Nachman's passing. At times, his life was in actual danger. As a result of this persecution, Reb Noson suffered loss of income, personal abuse, imprisonment and, eventually, three years of forced exile. Yet, through it all, he repeatedly writes in his letters to his followers, "Although we suffer, God has always favored us with His kindness. We have merited seeing much good granted us by God, even in the midst of our terrible distress."

What did Reb Noson mean by "God favored us with His kindness"? His enemies wanted to have him exiled to Siberia, but he was exiled only to a nearby city. His opponents tried to stop the spread of Rebbe Nachman's writings, yet Reb Noson was able to teach. Though his persecutors did what they could to prevent him from receiving financial support, Reb Noson was helped by several of his followers and was able to get by. For each instance, he credits God's kindness for his ability to survive despite the overwhelming opposition.

Difficulties are hard. Difficulties are frustrating. But difficulties are not a reason to throw up our hands and give up on God—or ourselves. For difficulties are nothing more than a spiritual elevator that takes us higher and higher.

WHAT DOES THIS MEAN TO ME ?

Every single person possesses deep reservoirs of inner strength that he or she can tap into when life gets difficult. How do we know this? Histories and biographies are full of stories of regular, everyday people who had their backs to the wall, people forced into the worst situations, who nevertheless managed to bounce back and survive. These people succeeded because they didn't give up when difficulties assailed them. Neither should we.

For Rebbe Nachman, one of the most difficult times in his life was two months before he passed away from tuberculosis. For three years, the disease ravaged his body and drained him physically on a daily basis. At that moment when all seemed dark and all the moods blackened with despair, he gave his famous call: "There is no such thing as despair!" "*Gevalt! Zeit aich nit meya'esh!—Gevalt!* Never allow yourselves to give up!" (see *Likutey Moharan* II, 78:7).

Reb Noson writes that Rebbe Nachman said these words with great strength and with deep feeling, proclaiming to all that there is never a reason for despair. You can always find at least a ray of God's infinite kindness, and you can always experience a glimmer of His endless compassion. You can always find God wherever you look for Him.

So the next time you're confronted by difficulties, large or small, remember Rebbe Nachman's call: "Never despair! Never give up!" Close your eyes, take a deep breath, and consider your options—because you do have them. Say a prayer to God to help you succeed in this situation He's put you into. Even if all the exits seem blocked, use your inner strength to cope with situations you cannot change.

Our souls are a part of God; it is His "breath," as it were, that breathes life into us at all times. Being aware that you are in God's presence can give you that extra lift in times of need and imbue you with the necessary strength to forge ahead.

This is as Rebbe Nachman said: "God is always with you. He is near you! He is next to you! Do not be afraid!" (*Siach Sarfey Kodesh* III, #661).

11

WHAT ARE THE GOOD POINTS?

God's way is to focus on the good. Even if there are things that aren't so good, He looks only for the good. How much more do we have to avoid focusing on the faults of our friends? We are obligated to seek only the good—always! (Likutey Moharan II, 17).

MORE THAN ANY other generation, 21st-century man is plagued by low self-esteem. Despite all our achievements in science and technology, a high standard of living and free education, most people are not happy. They think that the next gadget, the next vacation or the next home-redecorating project will do the trick, and they go for that...but still they're unhappy. Depression and suicide are at an all-time high. Is there any way out?

Yes, says Rebbe Nachman. The very fact that you are alive shows that you are of utmost importance. God loves you. He loves you as if you are His only child. You are the apple of His eye. Our Sages teach, "Every person must say, 'The world was created for me'" (*Sanhedrin* 37a). This means that I am the reason why God created the entire world. I must have worth. I am important, and I can be the good person that I aspire to be.

We actually have the power to raise ourselves and others to our position of true importance. In one of his most important lessons, called *Azamra!* (I Will Sing!),* Rebbe Nachman explains that if we look for the good in others, we can even elevate a sinner to the side of merit. How does this work? It means looking and searching for the teensiest bit of good that a person has ever done—be it holding open a door for an old lady or giving a penny to charity—and then looking for another bit, and another. By keeping at it, we can bring merit to anyone—even ourselves.

The faculty of judgment is one of man's most powerful tools. If we really knew just how powerful, we would certainly be more careful about how we use it. Elsewhere Rebbe Nachman teaches that judging others can destroy the world. If a person finds fault with another, this judgment can condemn the condemner (*Likutey Moharan* I, 3). Think about it! Your evaluation, opinion and judgment of others has the power to either elevate you or degrade you.

The problem is that criticism comes easy—too easy. We can always find fault in what others do or fail to do. Or as a friend of mine once said, "If only we were as quick to praise and thank our wives and other family members as we are to criticize them when things aren't what we expected!" If, in our judgment, we find the good points and focus on the positive, we can bring the entire world to the side of merit and worthiness. But if we find fault and focus on the negative, we can bring the entire world to the side of demerit and unworthiness. This is why we must always try to look for the good in others,

---

* This lesson is developed at length in a separate publication, *Azamra!* published by the Breslov Research Institute.

even in the worst person we know. Such emphasis on positive traits affects each person, as Rebbe Nachman teaches, "Favorable judgment actually elevates a person to the side of merit."

"But what about myself? I know what makes me tick. And believe me, there's no way—no way!—that I can honestly say that I'm okay, too." Too often we come down very hard on ourselves. "I'm no good! I messed up! Look what I did, again! Idiot that I am!" and so on. We become angry instead of tranquil. We become agitated instead of confident and controlled. Not the best way to be happy, or to strive for goals and accomplishments.

Even people who on the outside seem self-confident and generally positive about themselves, when pressed, will admit that they find it hard to judge themselves favorably. They know themselves too well and, basically, their self-evaluation may be accurate. Their good deeds may be driven by ulterior motives and improper thoughts. Yet within their flawed behavior there must be *some* good, some positive aspect. They should focus on that good, find another, then another—until they elevate themselves to the side of merit.

WHAT DOES THIS MEAN TO ME ?

One of the main reasons people get depressed is failure. A business deal you're working on falls through, a relationship you're trying to develop doesn't work out. "I've failed again," you tell yourself. Stop right there! Being pessimistic just opens the door to further failures. What else can you do? You can find a good point. Recharge yourself with optimism and positive thinking. You do have valuable qualities! You can succeed! Adopting this attitude will help you recover from any setback. Even in those areas where things were going all wrong, you'll encounter success.

Reb Noson not only studied Rebbe Nachman's teachings, he lived them. He translates the lesson of *Azamra!* into practical guidance for better relationships with family, friends and neighbors—indeed, with whoever we come in contact. Imagine, a majority of all arguments in the home (the most common and often the most harmful form of disagreement) would be eliminated instantly if only we could get ourselves to see the good points and focus only on the positive qualities in our spouses and children. Focusing on the good will turn your life into a purposeful life, a responsible life, a life of contentment and fulfillment. In short, if you are always looking for good, you will draw goodness and kindness into your life.

While you're looking for the good points, you might be surprised by just how many you discover. Reb Noson explains that whenever someone loses something important, he goes looking for it. He searches high and low, and eventually he finds it. Often, in the course of the search, he comes across other "lost" items, things he'd "forgotten" about and didn't remember that he still had. It's the same for someone who looks for his good points. In the course of his search, he inevitably comes across other "long-lost" tidbits that are his and his alone. Much to his surprise, he finds that he has a lot of "little good qualities" within him (*Likutey Halakhot, Birkhot HaPeirot* 5:4).

Once a fire swept through part of the town of Breslov. Passing by the site, Reb Noson and his followers spotted one of the distraught homeowners. Although crying bitterly, he was sifting through the rubble of his destroyed house in the hope of finding something, anything, that he might use to rebuild his home.

Reb Noson said, "Do you see what he's doing? Even though his house has been destroyed, he hasn't given up hope. He's collecting whatever might be useful for rebuilding. The same is true when it comes to spirituality and even emotional stability. The evil inclination fights against us, trying to destroy whatever holiness we've built up by getting us to do something that goes against God's will. Even so, when we are knocked down and all seems hopeless, we must never give up hope. We have to pick up a few good points and collect them together from amid the sins. This is *the* way to draw close to God" (*Kokhavey Or*, p. 78).

12

WHAT IS STARTING ANEW?

The essence of living is to begin anew each day. Chai (Hebrew for "living") also means "fresh" (*Likutey Halakhot, Basar b'Chalav* 4:12).

MEMORY MAKES US HUMAN. If we didn't have a memory, we would wake up each morning without recalling who we are or what we're doing in this world. Come to think of it, that might not be such a bad idea.

In Rebbe Nachman's worldview, every day is like a clean slate, a chance to start anew. Because we have the ability to forget, we can leave all our bad decisions and embarrassing mistakes where they belong—in the past. Now we can approach our work, our hobbies and our relationships with other people and with God with freshness and zest.

"Most people think of forgetting as a serious drawback," Rebbe Nachman explains. "But to me, it has a great advantage. If you did not forget, it would be utterly impossible to serve God. You would remember your entire past, and these memories would drag you down and not allow you to raise yourself to God. Whatever you did would be constantly disturbed by your memories of the past. The past is gone forever and never need be brought to mind. Because you can forget, you are no longer disturbed by the past."

Most people are distressed by past events—a slip of the tongue, a humiliating situation, an angry retort. We're also embarrassed by the serious mistakes we've made, whether financial, emotional or even accidental, such as breaking an arm. "What if...?" becomes the normal mindset and we never seem to extricate ourselves from the merry-go-round of thoughts like, "What if I had done this?" or, "If only I had said that."

The litany of worries over whether we did something wrong or neglected something important interferes with getting things done in the here and now. It affects our ability to form new relationships ("What if I say something stupid like I did last time?"), pursue new business opportunities ("If they find out how I messed up before, they won't want to work with me"), and even pray to God properly ("Why should God listen to me when I have so many sins and shortcomings?"). The best advice for putting these worries to rest is simply to forget. As soon as an event is over with, says Rebbe Nachman, forget it completely and never think about it again.

Of course we do have an obligation to make amends for our past misdeeds. With the help of a rabbi or spiritual mentor, we can embark on a program of *teshuvah* (repentance) to rectify any moral failings we've had vis-a-vis God or our fellow Jews. But we shouldn't let our past failings cripple us with self-recrimination and second-guessing. We can start anew, every day!

In the future, God will let everyone remember everything, even if it was forgotten during his lifetime (see

Zohar I, 185a). This is also true of all of life's lessons that a person heard but didn't understand. In the World to Come, everything will be comprehended (*Tzaddik* #388).

WHAT DOES THIS MEAN TO ME?

Nothing weighs down a person more than worrying about past actions that he can never take back or change. The secret to dumping that "excess baggage" and making a success of our lives is to forget the past and start anew. We should acknowledge that we are human, we are subject to error, and yet we can move on and accomplish bigger and better things. And we are precious enough in God's sight that He will always accept us whenever we return to Him.

Therefore, make every day count. Allow yourself to look forward to a life of accomplishment and joy. When you awake in the morning or plan your schedule, anticipate the positive ways you can conduct your professional and personal activities. Think of ways to improve your relationships and even put aside old grudges. When new opportunities present themselves, try approaching them with the excitement and creativity you always wished you had.

Starting anew gives you the courage to take chances and be an "original." Despite my shortcomings and past failures, I can be a new person, I can be original in my approach. But I never tried this or did this before? No matter. Today I can start anew (see *Likutey Moharan* I, 272). Rebbe Nachman once said about himself, "That a single word does not leave my lips without some innovation—that goes without saying. But not even a breath leaves my lips without originality!" (*Tzaddik* #384).

Also, take time to recall all the joy and good you've ever experienced. That is using memory at its best and fosters positive thinking and creativity. It also helps you draw on your inner reserves of strength, always hoping for the good to emerge.

Rebbe Nachman teaches that every morning upon arising, a person should immediately "recall" the World to Come (*Likutey Moharan* I, 54:2). By focusing on the true goal of life in this world—the reward for our good deeds that awaits us in the World to Come—we can overlook and even forget the frivolities of this world. We can add that this is a reason why we recite the *Modeh Ani* (I Thank You) prayer upon awakening. Singing God's praises first thing in the morning focuses our attention and builds our anticipation for the true good that lies in store for us!

13

WHAT IS TRUTH?

Truth will sprout from the earth (Psalms 85:11).

Reb Noson once remarked on this verse: Planted seeds must be nurtured, guarded and watered in order to grow properly. So too, truth must be carefully guarded and nurtured so that when it sprouts, it will emerge in its perfected form (Ma'asiyot u'Meshalim, p. 40).

TRUTH IS A WONDERFUL IDEAL. But just start talking to a few people and you'll begin to wonder where the truth really lies. Everyone believes his idea is the correct one and her solution is the right one! We tend to see things from our own perspective, and that is *my* truth. But then the other person sees things from his perspective, which is *his* truth. The problem with truth is that it can be only one thing: the truth!

Rebbe Nachman explains that there are many lies, but there is only one truth. You can call a silver cup, "a silver cup." That's the truth. But if you use any other description, like "a gold cup," "a copper cup," or "a paper cup," it's not the truth. Either it is what it is, or it isn't. That's the truth.

So the truth is always one. But each person has a different perspective of truth, which stems from the fact that God, Who is One, created each of us differently. Since each of us is very different from the next person, we each have varying perspectives of the truth.

Reb Noson explains that since each of us sees things differently, then we *all* have truth, which is why we can each present our views truthfully. The real problems arise when we do not accept the validity of another person's view—which, according to him, is also the truth. Then strife enters the picture: as each person stands on his perspectives, the gaps between people become wider and more diversified.

This is the origin of all the arguments that exist in the world. Each person "knows" he is right and that automatically and by extension the other cannot be right. Or as Rebbe Nachman says, "The characteristic of victory does not allow for truth. To prove his point, a person will never allow another view to enter his mind" (see *Likutey Moharan* I, 122).

Our insistence on the truth—"our" truth—actually brings about the negation of truth, along with strife and the accompanying falsehoods, misrepresentations and rationalizations that distance us from the truth even more. For when we try to embellish the truth, or adapt it or anything else, we enter into distortions and lies, and we can actually sink into horrific quagmires. What's most frightening is that we do it to ourselves!

It might be that little white lie that we said in order to protect ourselves from embarrassment. It might be a little "alteration" that we added to the story so that we look good in other people's eyes. Or it might be a whopping tale to save our job, our marriage, or whatever else feels important to us. No matter how you cloak it, it's a falsehood. (Our Sages teach that for the sake of peace, one is permitted to change his story [*Yevamot* 65b]. But one must be careful with the alterations, lest he fool himself, too!)

Notice how little effort it takes. After all, it's just a few words. But let's compare it to highway driving. You're on the expressway and take the wrong exit. Now you're lost and trying to get back on the right road. But you take a wrong turn, then another and another. You lose time, you lose patience; frankly, you're off the path and whatever happens, you're lost.

Truth is God and truth is light, the proper and illuminated path. Any veering from that path leads a person astray. If we distort that path even a little, it will lead us to many other and different pathways in life that prove disastrous. Rebbe Nachman teaches that falsehood damages one's sight, physically and spiritually (*Likutey Moharan* I, 51). A lie can damage one's sight so that he does not see the consequences of his words or actions. This leads him to say things that are harmful to himself or to others. Another falsehood can "blind" the person and the chances of error increases manifold.

Someone pointed out to Reb Noson a leading *maskil* (follower of the Enlightenment movement) in town who left the path of Judaism. Yet this person never, ever, told a lie. "See how honest and upstanding he is?" he said. Reb Noson replied, "Maybe he never tells a lie. But he is living a lie!" (*Oral tradition*). Truth and falsehood have their individual values and purposes. But as Reb Noson is implying, be careful how you use them. They can make—or break—your life.

WHAT DOES THIS MEAN TO ME ?

Rebbe Nachman and Reb Noson often speak about truth and how we must seek it at all times. The way to go about this is to seek "its face."

Everything is identifiable by its face. Just as you would identify a person or an item by looking directly at it, look at yourself and your actions with absolute honesty. Ask yourself, "Is this who I really am, or is this just a face that I present to those around me?" "What is it that I really want out of life?" And, "What am I prepared to do to make myself a better person?" Truth is readily definable, as long as we look it straight in the face. We have to be willing to seek and search for what truth is and then, when we see it, to accept it (even if it's not to our liking it at first). It is, after all, the truth.

Have you ever said, "I don't need that extra piece of cake"—and then gone ahead and eaten it anyway? Have you ever told yourself, "I can't afford that"—and then booked that luxury vacation or bought that expensive car? Being honest with yourself doesn't mean never indulging, but you must go in with both eyes open and be ready to face the consequences of your decisions.

In the physical realm, being honest with yourself means taking care of your body, not eating to excess or consuming unhealthy foods, and avoiding drugs. It means exercising and doing things that are beneficial for your body. That is being honest. The simple reason is that the body cloaks the soul and without proper maintenance, the soul cannot serve God.

The same idea of honesty applies to the emotional realm. When we're upset with a child, we may get angry or even fly into a rage. But to what benefit? What can be gained by anger? What will the child learn from it? The same applies to husband-wife relationships and dealings with siblings, friends and coworkers. Do we choose hate over love, depression over joy, obsession over calm? If we get into the habit of always asking ourselves, "What is the necessity or reality of this?" then we are being honest with ourselves.

Honesty is most important in the spiritual realm. No one will know if you're just acting the part except you—and God. Ask yourself, "Are my prayers up to par? Am I really striving to have a relationship with God? Or am I a creature of habit, without feeling any life or emotion in my devotions?"

Without honesty, there is no growth—physically, emotionally, spiritually or financially. But when we look for truth, we are taking a "reality check" at just about every step, and know in which direction we're headed in all of life's challenges.

When we bring truth into our lives, we draw light into our lives. And, by association, we draw God into our lives! (see *Likutey Moharan* I, 9:3). Our whole outlook changes as we redirect our perspective to a higher and deeper level. Truth is the foundation on which all else depends.

14

WHAT IS FAITH?

Rebbe Nachman teaches: Faith is like a beautiful palace with many beautiful rooms. One enters and wanders about from room to room, from hallway to hallway... From there one walks on in trust...then further and further. How fortunate is he who walks in faith! (Tzaddik #420).

Rebbe Nachman said, "Others consider faith a minor thing. But I consider it an extremely great thing" (Rabbi Nachman's Wisdom #33). *When the Rebbe told Reb Noson to record his own discourses, he said to him, "In your writings, every word should be measured. But when you come to the topic of faith, let your pen flow!"* (Rabbi Eliyahu Chaim Rosen). *The importance of faith is unparalleled. Without it, we cannot enter the realm of spirituality. With it, we can attain the highest of levels.*

FAITH IS THE FOUNDATION of the world. More specifically, it is *the* fundamental principle of Judaism, Torah, and even of humanity itself. At the beginning of time God placed faith into all of Creation, as it is written, "All His work is with faithfulness" (Psalms 33:4). Therefore, there is no one alive who doesn't have faith in something or someone, and throughout life we are constantly being asked to corroborate that faith: "Do I have faith in my spouse, my neighbor, my child, my grocer, my stockbroker? Are they deserving of my trust?"

All business is ultimately conducted through faith. When examining merchandise you're interested in purchasing, you ask the price. Do you buy it? If you believe that the merchant's price is fair, you do. If you suspect there's something wrong or you simply don't trust the merchant, you don't. Even chairmen of multinational conglomerates must place their faith in their assistants' reports, in the work of people they trust. We can't survive in this world without the attribute of faith.

Generally speaking, the term "faith" applies to what we do not know or cannot understand. We do not need faith to say that the four-legged piece of wood in front of us is a table, or that the four walls surrounding us form a room. We see it. We know it. And we do not need faith to be convinced that if we stick our finger in a fire, we're going to get burned. We feel it. We know it. Faith becomes necessary only when we cannot directly experience the object with our senses or understand the reason for doing something.

This easily applies to our relationship with God, Who is beyond us and right next to us at the same time. Rebbe Nachman teaches that there's a glorious world out there—and a super-benevolent God in charge of it all. But He conceals His presence from us to give us free will. If we remain steadfast in our faith in Him, then as soon as we pierce the veil and say, "I know you're there, God! I believe in you!" then all the concealments fall away and we feel God as never before.

But this faith must be nurtured. We've been tested

again and again, and we will be tested again in the future. The whole world is really a testing ground in which obstacles and challenges exist solely to see how we will respond and what choices we will make. Sometimes the tests are financial, sometimes physical, and at other times our emotions are put on the chopping block. And our spirituality is continually bombarded by outside influences that challenge the very core of our beliefs.

> Rebbe Nachman once encouraged a man who was greatly confused about his beliefs. The Rebbe told him, "All of creation came into being only because of people like you. God saw that there would be people who would cling to our holy faith, despite suffering greatly because of the confusion and doubts that constantly plague them. He perceived that they would overcome these doubts and strengthen themselves in their beliefs. It was because of this that God brought forth all creation." After hearing this, the man was greatly strengthened and unperturbed whenever he had these confusing thoughts (*Rabbi Nachman's Wisdom* #222).

Having faith is one thing. Keeping it is another. But we have to have faith anyway, as mentioned above, since somewhere along the way we require faith. If so, Rebbe Nachman is teaching us to always strengthen ourselves in faith. It can be done. And it is most rewarding.

Even if we don't understand it fully, it will become clear later on. Reb Noson explains that faith and knowledge are two sides of the same coin. We begin with faith, which eventually culminates with knowledge and understanding of what we believe in. With this understanding, we are ready to make the next leap of faith to ascend to a higher level of faith! (*Likutey Halakhot, Cheilev vaDam* 4:2).

WHAT DOES THIS MEAN TO ME ?

With faith, one has a life. Whatever goes wrong, the person has consolation in knowing that God is behind it and he can take solace in His Creator. He also has hope and faith that everything is for the best and will eventually turn out good. On the other hand, without faith, where does a person turn in time of need? In times of trouble? (see *Rabbi Nachman's Wisdom* #51, #101).

Reb Noson lists four types of faith that we should try to cultivate:

- Faith in God
- Faith in the Torah
- Faith in the Tzaddikim
- Faith in yourself

FAITH IN GOD means believing that He exists, He is Omnipotent, He guides the world with Divine Providence and oversees all that is happening. Someone as All-Powerful as God certainly has the power to grant your requests and prayers. But you have to believe it! Otherwise your prayers won't be nearly as effective. How will you ever establish a relationship with God if you don't have that kind of faith in Him?

FAITH IN THE TORAH means believing that the Torah provides us with the correct parameters for dealing with life. For this reason, we must place great emphasis on simply observing Torah laws. By having faith in Torah and *mitzvot*, we will begin to understand the importance of following the Torah and see the positive influence it has on our lives.

On the other hand, abandoning faith in the Torah—

and especially the Oral Law—leads to catastrophic results. Throughout Jewish history, breakaway sects have caused many difficulties for the Jewish people. These include the idolaters during the First Temple, the Sadducees of the Second Temple, the Karaites in the Geonic period (beginning around 600 C.E.), the apostates of the medieval era, and groups up to our own day that choose to negate the Oral Law. Yet rather than spawn new movements with lots of followers, these splinter groups inevitably die out, because they are detached from the Torah, the source of life (see *Likutey Halakhot, Halva'ah* 4:8).

FAITH IN THE TZADDIKIM means placing our trust in the unique individuals in each generation who achieve great levels of piety in their relationship to God, and are thus able to bring God's word back to those of lower spiritual consciousness (see Chapter 17, "What is the Tzaddik?"). In fact, the Tzaddikim are such lofty examples of religious devotion and moral purity that God often lets them be the conduit for blessing to the world.

FAITH IN YOURSELF is so important that without it, the other three areas of faith will always be lacking. Reb Noson explains that self-faith involves:

- Believing that I, as an individual, am very important in God's eyes.
- Believing that no matter how far I may be from God, I have the power to return to Him.
- Believing that no matter how I presently conduct my life, I have the inner strength to change my habits.
- Believing that I have the self-confidence to deal with others.

• Believing that I, too, have the ability to become a Tzaddik.

Rebbe Nachman teaches that an important practice in strengthening self-faith is to repeat over and over, "I believe in God!" as in the verse, "I will make known Your faith with my mouth" (Psalms 89:2; *Likutey Moharan* II, 44).

Armed with faith—in God, in the Torah, in the Tzaddikim and in ourselves—we can always find an outlet for our emotions and feelings, and always find ways to better ourselves and repair any wrongdoings of the past. We can face the future with confidence, knowing that we stand on the solid foundation of faith.

15

WHAT IS THE COVENANT?

The main way to draw close to God is by guarding the covenant (Likutey Moharan I, 29:4).

THE COVENANT, OR *BRIT*, refers to the pact that God made with Abraham, the first patriarch of the Jewish people. God said, "This is My covenant that you will keep, between Me and you and your children after you: Every male must be circumcised" (Genesis 17:10). The mitzvah of circumcision is the sign of the deal that God made with Abraham and his future offspring, the Jewish people. God promised to be true to the Jewish people, never abandoning them for another nation, and the Jewish people, in turn, promised to be true to God. Unlike a business deal, where if one side pulls out, the other side is absolved of its commitment, a covenant is eternal. Even if the Jewish people renege on their promise (which, unfortunately, they did several times in their history, opting to serve idols rather than God), God will never back out on His end of the deal.

We see that despite their occasional lapses in faithfulness to God, the Jews have always kept the mitzvah of *brit milah* (literally, "covenant of circumcision") no matter

REBBE NACHMAN AND YOU

what. Many nations—ancient Greece, ancient Rome, Spain during the Inquisition, Nazi Germany—tried to force the Jews to give up this practice, but they held on tenaciously, showing their willingness to be killed rather than forsake the covenant. Even today, as secularism has swept through the ranks of world Jewry and left many ignorant of the most basic tenets of our tradition, circumcision is still one thing that all Jewish boys have in common. Deep down, a Jew senses his unique connection to God (see *Shabbat* 130a).

The great medieval commentator Rashi explains that the sign of the covenant was established in a place where one can differentiate between male and female (Rashi on Genesis 17:14). On a deeper level, the sign of the covenant teaches us that parameters should be set between male and female. When these parameters are honored and guarded, a special relationship of mutual honor and respect evolves between a married couple.

Marriage and fidelity to one partner are seen as almost a joke in contemporary society. "Why wait?" and "Just do it" are the mantras of the sexual gurus of the modern age. A man would have to be blind not to notice the skimpy new fashions, the suggestive pictures in print and online media, and the alluring music that blares from every car and shop. Sex is seen as a casual thing, something to try on and discard like a pair of socks. It's no wonder that by the time young men and women decide to get married, their heads are filled with so much trash and indecency that they find it hard to concentrate on their spouse and his or her needs.

Our Sages refer to marriage as *KiDuShin* (קידושין), from the Hebrew word *KoDeSH* (קדש), "holy." The union between husband and wife is meant to be an act of respect, endearment and holiness. When the couple focuses on each other to the exclusion of all others, the Divine Presence resides between them (cf. *Sotah* 17a). That is, a certain karma can be felt in their home that allows peace and harmony to exist and affects all the members of the household. The sanctity of attitude towards the relationship heightens one's awareness of one's mate.

The organ on which the *brit milah* is performed has another, even more important function: the ability to initiate new life. This is the reason God commanded Abraham to perform a circumcision on himself before he fathered Isaac, so that Isaac would be born in a state of holiness. The *Zohar* emphasizes that the thoughts and attitudes of the parents at the time of the marital act have a very telling effect on the child that will be conceived (*Zohar Chadash* 15a). Rebbe Nachman adds that by sanctifying the marital act, the parents can draw a bright and illumined soul to their child, a soul that contributes to the child's greater development, growth and abilities in later years (*Likutey Moharan* I, 14:4). Unfortunately, the reverse is also true.

The importance of guarding the covenant plays a major role in Rebbe Nachman's teachings. Someone who does not guard his sexual purity, but indulges in every lust and pleasure that the world has to offer, will never be able to have a successful relationship with God, Who represents the ultimate in holiness and purity. This is as the verse states, "Speak to the Children of Israel and say to them, 'Be holy, because I, God your Lord, am holy'" (Leviticus 19:2). The *Zohar* (II, 3b) refers to a blemish of the covenant as a "lie," because that person has lied to God in his relationship with Him; he has taken the God-given power of creating life and used it falsely, in a wrongful relationship. If you want Godliness, you can't indulge in every lust. It's that simple.

Rebbe Nachman explains that there are three levels of existence: sanctity, purity and impurity (*Likutey Moharan* I, 51:2). We live in an impure world where all types of lust surround us. We can either give in and become impure like our environment, or we can strive for the sanctified. And know that there exists a path that is very close to sanctity yet allows a person to have his cake and eat it, too. That is the level of purity. As long as we control our desires, we fulfill the teaching, "Sanctify yourself with what is permitted" (*Yevamot* 20a).

Rebbe Nachman says, "All Jews are called Tzaddikim in that they are circumcised" (*Likutey Moharan* I, 23:10). The merit of the covenant of circumcision is very great; it is enough to earn a Jew the distinction of holiness and the accolade of Tzaddik. The Tzaddik is the epitome of sexual morality and, as a result, has a closer relationship to God than the average person. Just as the Tzaddik has the special power to raise all those around him, bringing them to a heightened awareness of God and His teachings, a person who guards his covenant can raise himself and many others to a heightened awareness of honesty, decency and purity.

One who makes the effort to guard his covenant shows what he considers important in life and displays his fortitude in following through on his claims and intentions. Such a person attains honor and respect (cf. ibid., I, 11:3); he is also more open to earn a better livelihood, since he exudes a sense of honesty and trustworthiness (cf. ibid., I, 29:5). By guarding the covenant, he also merits peace; there's no web of lies to weave around the life he leads (cf. ibid., I, 33:1).

It's not easy—not at all. But being able to walk around with your head held high, radiating goodness and trustworthiness, will make you feel good about yourself your entire life.

WHAT DOES THIS MEAN TO ME ?

Guarding the covenant means living with focus, clarity and purpose. Instead of being bombarded by sights and sounds that drag us to places we never thought we'd go, we are in control. We can choose what to do and reap the benefits of those decisions in terms of more holiness and more purity. Though we may fear that we will "turn into a monk" if so many casual relationships are proscribed to us, the opposite is true. When we commit to one person, investing all our focus and desire into that one spouse alone, we will find it even more liberating and satisfying because of unity of purpose.

Rebbe Nachman's approach to guarding the covenant makes it very simple for us. There are things that are permitted, and there are things that are forbidden. There are also temptations that crop up and can lead us on an immoral road and way of life. When we concentrate on doing everything it takes to guard our covenant, we will automatically live a life of morality. As we do so, we will automatically be drawing closer to God and earning His blessing.

These specific things are musts when it comes to guarding the covenant:

- Marrying someone who is Jewish
- Avoiding sexual relations with a menstruating woman

- Avoiding extramarital affairs
- Avoiding homosexual relationships
- Refraining from masturbation
- Guarding one's eyes from indecent pictures and displays

The last item on the list may come as a surprise. If I'm working so hard on having the right relationships and avoiding the wrong ones, why can't I take a peek now and then? I promise nothing will happen!

Are you sure? The eyes are the windows to the world. This means that the way a person looks at things is the way they will be transmitted to his mind and, in turn, become the director of his actions. By internalizing lust, we fill our minds with thoughts that aren't healthy, for the mind as well as for the body. Our Sages teach that the seed is drawn from the entire body and the more it is spent, the greater the toll it takes on the body by weakening it (cf. *Niddah* 43a; see *Orach Chaim* 240:14). Physiologically speaking, by guarding the eyes and acting in a way that is morally correct, a person protects and sustains his bodily fluids so that his "natural juices" remain until a ripe old age.

So it develops that guarding the covenant is helpful to one's physical well-being as well as mental stability. It leads to a moral life, a firmness of resolve, the ability to see things through to their conclusion (because one has a solid foundation), and reliability in all facets of life. And when we realize that the covenant parallels the *sefirah* of *Yesod* (see Charts, p. 183), it takes on a whole new meaning. The Hebrew word *Yesod* means "Foundation." Living morally means building a solid foundation for one's entire life.

16

WHAT IS A TIKKUN?

If you believe it is possible to destroy, believe it is possible to repair (*Likutey Moharan* II, 112).

ALL IS FINE AND GOOD if one can maintain a moral life. But what if a person fails or succumbs to temptation when trying to pray, to avoid non-kosher food, or to guard the covenant? Is there any hope? Can he ever rectify what he did wrong?

Just as in "real life," mistakes are made that must be corrected, so too, in spiritual life, errors are made and, sometimes, God forbid, even intentional sins are committed. The ARI speaks of the damage caused by sin, which empowers the forces of evil and is the source of all suffering—illness, natural disasters and all kinds of damage. Is there a way to fix these, too?

The answer, says Rebbe Nachman, is a resounding "YES!"

The Hebrew word *TiKkuN* (תקון) means "repair," "rectification," and "preparation." *LeTaKeiN ma'akhalim* means to prepare food (for a meal); we perform various other *tikkunim* to prepare ourselves for the day ahead, like brushing our teeth and taking that daily dose of caffeine in our morning coffee. The rest of our day appears to be filled with *tikkunim*, in terms of both preparing for and fixing what goes wrong at the office, on our errands and in our personal relationships. What about *tikkunim* in the spiritual realm?

Rebbe Nachman speaks often of *tikkunim*. He speaks of *tikkunim* for souls, he speaks of repentance as a *tikkun* for sin, and he revealed the *Tikkun HaKlali*, the General Remedy, which he explains as a general *tikkun* that can effect rectification for any and all individual blemishes (*Likutey Moharan* I, 29:3). Rebbe Nachman always holds out hope even for someone who committed the worst acts, and states emphatically that one can always repent and return to God. Always. Even from the worst sins, even from the lowest levels. Surprisingly, Reb Noson adds that Rebbe Nachman taught that sometimes a person's sins are so powerful that when he recognizes his folly, that very recognition leads him to repentance. Then, everything he did wrong can be transformed into *mitzvot*! (see *Likutey Halakhot, Birkhot HaRei'ach* 4:2).

God is always with us; He permeates every nanometer of existence. When we seek Him, we're bound to find Him, somewhere, somehow. But when we err (or worse), we lose that contact, much as a person who makes a wrong turn ends up in unfamiliar territory. Our Sages say, "When a person sins and then repeats the sin, he begins to think it's permissible" (*Kiddushin* 20a). Then he asks, "Where is God?" I might not see Him or feel Him, so I am distant. Can I ever return to Him?

Rebbe Nachman teaches that at that very first moment when a person thinks of God, saying, "God! Where are You?" he immediately connects with God and can now begin his return to Him. For although he may think that he is eons distant from God, God is really right next to him! He just wasn't aware of it. But the minute he calls out, "God! Where are You?" he makes contact and will find that God is with him at all times, in all places, even in the filthiest of places, even in the worst situations (*Likutey Moharan* II, 12).

This idea applies to everything a person has ever done throughout his entire life. We can always call out to God from wherever we are. Rebbe Nachman said, "God is always with you. He is near you! He is next to you! Do not be afraid!" (*Siach Sarfey Kodesh* III, #661). This applies to every misdeed, every wrongful act, every evil thought and every wrongful word. And we may be pleasantly surprised by the outcome. Our Sages teach, "When a person repents out of fear of God, then his sins are re-evaluated from intentional sins and are calculated only as accidental sins. But when a person returns to God out of love, then all his sins are transformed into good deeds!" (*Yoma* 86b).

How can that be? Transforming sins into good deeds? But when one serves God out of love, he invokes the attribute of *AHaVaH* (אהבה), "love," which in Hebrew has the same numerical value (13) as *EChaD* (אחד), "one." All becomes a unity, all becomes one—one with God.

This is what is meant by a *tikkun*. A person can fix many things. It begins with his repentance, his turning towards God, which has a tremendous effect on mini-mizing or even completely erasing his sins. A *tikkun* is the means of rectifying what we did wrong. It is some-thing we can do, it is something we must do. And it is something that Rebbe Nachman taught us is in our power to effect!

WHAT DOES THIS MEAN TO ME ?

Rare is the person who goes through life without inadvertently saying the wrong thing—some gossip (or slander), mockery, profanity, that little white lie (or the big whopper), flattery, and so on. How about getting angry and embarrassing others? When it comes to *mitzvot* like observing Shabbat and Jewish festivals, how many people are so well-versed in the laws, bylaws and additional subsections to the laws of these holy days that they can say they never transgressed any of them? Then there are those who succumb to temptation and eat something forbidden or commit a sexual sin, whether of thought, word or deed. How can we fix those mistakes?

We all know that a sin can be erased through repentance. But the holy writings question how this works, since a sin might have been committed in a certain place at a certain time, and now, years later, the person is far from the "scene of the crime" in both time and place. For example, an employer was incensed at a secretary and humiliated her in front of the whole office. The secretary quit and moved to a faraway city. Years later, the boss wants to rectify what was said or done wrong, but has no idea where the secretary lives. What if she's no longer alive? Can that sin ever be erased?

Rebbe Nachman teaches that yes, each person can effect a *tikkun* for his sins. There are ways and means that a person can turn to God to effect rectification, though some cases are more difficult than others. Still, it is possible, depending on the level of regret and repentance. It needs some effort, crying and begging

God for forgiveness, but it can be done. A problem does develop when another person is involved—for example, if we embarrass someone or speak slander against him—for then we must ask forgiveness from him, too. Even if that person has moved far away or passed away, we can still effect forgiveness. If a person asks enough, God will see to it that the injured party will forgive.

Even sexual sin—and especially masturbation, which is considered the worst possible sin (see *Even HaEzer* 23:1)—can be rectified. Towards this, Rebbe Nachman said, "This sin has been with us since Adam (see *Eruvin* 18b). All the Tzaddikim throughout all the generations have worked on finding a rectification for this sin. God helped me and I totally grasped the solution. Rectifying this matter by reciting the Ten Psalms [the *Tikkun HaKlali*—see p. 114] is something completely new, an outstanding innovation, and a wonderful and awesome remedy". He explained that Psalms are comprised of the Ten Types of Song, which are the most powerful force to bring a person back to God (see *Rabbi Nachman's Wisdom* #141; *Rabbi Nachman's Stories* #13, the Sixth Day).

Many Breslover Chassidim make it a daily practice to say the *Tikkun HaKlali*. Their reason? If Rebbe Nachman taught that the *Tikkun HaKlali* helps to rectify even after a sin, how much more effective would it be if we recite the *Tikkun before* the sin! This practice can also work for you. The more we seek a *tikkun* for our wrongdoings, the greater our chances of making it happen.

But what if our repentance falls short, or we don't feel it's been effective? This is another reason why we need to be attached to the Tzaddikim (see Chapter 17, "What is the Tzaddik?"). The Tzaddikim are constantly seeking ways to rectify all sins, even the worst sins, and are always working to bring everyone to a state of perfection. When I turn to God and rely not on myself (who has erred) but on those Tzaddikim who were always righteous and know how to serve God, and I accept their teachings and try to follow their guidance, then even if I am found wanting, what else could I have done to rectify my ways? By attaching myself to the Tzaddikim, it is possible to repair everything. Literally everything!

Fortunate is the person who recognizes his errors and repents, thereby effecting rectification for his sins. For all of them!

17

WHAT IS THE TZADDIK?

The Tzaddik is the foundation of the world (Proverbs 10:25).

AT THE BEGINNING OF Creation, God created light and then differentiated between light and darkness (Genesis 1:4). Indeed, God created many opposing forces and gave man the free will to choose between them: to choose light over darkness, right over wrong, good over evil. God's purpose in Creation was for man to consider and define for himself the correct route to choose in every situation.

Though many attempt to follow the path of true righteousness, few succeed in overcoming the attractions and temptations of this world. God knew that this would be so. He knew that most men would succumb to temptation, some more, some less—but He also knew that a few would triumph and withstand all temptations. These few are the symbol of light and the epitome of what man can achieve.

The concept of the Tzaddik, or righteous individual, has always been a part of Judaism and appears throughout our holy writings. To wit:

- For the merit of even one Tzaddik, the world was created (*Yoma* 38b).
- God decrees and the Tzaddik has the power to nullify the decree. But, the Tzaddik decrees and God fulfills his decree (cf. *Mo'ed Katan* 16b).
- Not only are Tzaddikim able to nullify decrees, but they are afterwards blessed for this (*Zohar* I, 101b).
- If the Tzaddikim would so wish, they could create worlds (*Sanhedrin* 65b).
- Tzaddikim draw down and reveal God's Divine Presence in the world (*Shir HaShirim Rabbah* 5:1).

Some Tzaddikim are predestined for greatness from the time of Creation. Their righteousness—which in any case they have to establish through their own good deeds—is given to them so that they can perform a certain mission for God. Other individuals rise to the level of Tzaddik by overcoming their physical desires and devoting their entire lives to God. They earn the title on their own.

When someone suggested to Rebbe Nachman that he had achieved all that he did because of his exalted soul, the Rebbe seemed very annoyed. "This is the trouble. You think that Tzaddikim attain greatness merely because they have a very great soul. This is absolutely wrong! I worked very hard for all this. I put much effort into attaining what I did...it is because of the devotions and the efforts I put in" (*Rabbi Nachman's Wisdom* #165).

The best way to describe the Tzaddik is as a bridge between the physical and the spiritual. Having subdued his natural desires and negative character traits in his quest for holiness, he transcends the physical and is capable of grasping what spirituality is really about. With this mastery, he can take the most wondrous aspects of Godliness and bring them down to a level that the simplest person can relate to. Some Tzaddikim convey their knowledge to us through their teachings, others through their deeds. Observing the Tzaddikim, either through their spoken or written lessons, helps us understand what is important.

Because he has one foot in this world and one foot in Heaven, the Tzaddik is an intermediary between us and God. Of course, no Jew (or anyone else) needs an intermediary between himself and God, for he can always search for and seek out God, and he can find Him. But the Tzaddik has already found God and therefore, to put it simply, he knows the way to find God. This means he is the ideal leader and guide to teach us whatever we need to know for our own pursuit of Godliness.

Unfortunately, the term "intermediary" has been twisted and misused by those who do not, or cannot, understand who the Tzaddik is. They cast aspersions on and question the validity of his role. In doing so, they mislead people and draw them far away from the Tzaddik. This did not begin with the advent of Chassidic Tzaddikim. Already in biblical times we find that "the people mocked the messengers of God" (II Chronicles 36:16). These "messengers" were none other than the Tzaddikim and prophets of that generation. Then, as now, people had no conception of how great these leaders were. They thought themselves capable of choosing their leaders (as is done in "democratic" countries) and of knowing the correct path in life. This attitude caused the destruction of the Temple and the beginning of our long exile.

To avail ourselves of the guidance and direction that

the Tzaddik has to offer, we must "bind" ourselves to the Tzaddik. This means following the Tzaddik's example and accepting his advice. Rebbe Nachman explains that the key to achieving spirituality is listening to the Tzaddik—to everything that he says—and not deviating from it by an iota. Just accept his teachings with full faith and simplicity (*Likutey Moharan* I, 123). When we do what the Tzaddik says and as he does, we become attached to him spiritually, and then we ourselves become Tzaddik-like (ibid., I, 7:4). Thus, a person who follows his rabbi or Chassidic master becomes bound to that *rav*. Following Rebbe Nachman's advice attaches the follower to Rebbe Nachman.

Even after a Tzaddik passes away (such as in the case of Rebbe Nachman), one does not have to sever his relationship with the Tzaddik. For one who is completely holy, death as we know it has no effect over him (*Zohar* II, 174a). The Tzaddik's power and influence are even stronger after death, since his physical body no longer encumbers him.

For this reason, it is an ancient Jewish custom to visit the gravesites of Tzaddikim and pray there for God's salvation for personal difficulties as well as for the salvation of Israel (*Orach Chaim* 581:4). Among the graves of Tzaddikim with which you may be familiar are the graves of Rabbi Shimon bar Yochai in Meron, Rachel's Tomb outside Bethlehem, the Cave of Machpelah in Hebron where the Patriarchs are buried, King David's Tomb on Mount Zion, and the graves of many of the Talmudic rabbis located throughout Israel. The grave of one of most famous Tzaddikim, Moses, was hidden by God. The Talmud explains that if the location of Moses' grave was known to man, the Jews would go there to pray—and they would immediately be redeemed from exile! (*Sotah* 14a; *Eyn Yaakov, Sotah* #54).

• • •

REBBE NACHMAN TEACHES that there are many good and righteous Tzaddikim in this world. But in every generation, there is one unique individual called the True Tzaddik who is the real leader of the Jewish nation (see *Likutey Moharan* I, 66:4). He is there for everyone—for each person on his or her own level—and he can guide each individual on the path he or she needs to live a full life. This applies not only to spiritual living, but to physical, emotional and financial circumstances as well.

In the nascent days of the Jewish nation, the True Tzaddik was obviously Moses, who spoke with God directly and diligently taught His Torah to each and every Jew. Other leaders of exceptional caliber include Rabbi Akiva, Rashi, the ARI, the Baal Shem Tov, and so on. Breslover Chassidim consider Rebbe Nachman to be a True Tzaddik—not only for his generation, but for generations to come.

Ask anyone who has been touched by Rebbe Nachman's teachings what inspired him to study Breslov writings and he'll answer, "Rebbe Nachman speaks to me directly." One present-day Breslover summed it up this way: "I find it absolutely amazing that the words of someone who lived in the late 18th and early 19th centuries in Eastern Europe can, 200 years later, relate directly to someone such as myself, a product of 21st-century Western civilization." Rebbe Nachman's teachings are universal, covering the entire spectrum of Judaism. They maintain their freshness and are inspiring; they give hope and encouragement, assurance and motivation to anyone and everyone, from all walks of life.

Open any book of Rebbe Nachman's teachings and you'll find advice for countless situations. The Rebbe always seems to have something to say for what you're going through right now. Review that same material some time later, when other concerns occupy your thoughts, and you'll find in it an entirely new set of directions—advice specifically applicable to your new situation and circumstances. This is difficult to explain to anyone who has never studied Rebbe Nachman's works. His teachings are bottomless wellsprings, ever-flowing brooks of life and vitality. We need only avail ourselves of them to benefit from their amazing resources and counsel.

Rebbe Nachman said, "I am a river that cleanses from all stains" (*Tzaddik* #332). Whoever has taken the Rebbe's advice and spoken to God in *hitbodedut* (see p. 113) knows the wonderful sensation of being able to open his heart and pour out his innermost feelings. He knows that no matter where he is, God is with him, waiting for him to come closer. He also knows that no matter how bad things get in life, there is that reservoir of inner strength to rely upon, because Rebbe Nachman called out, "Never despair! There is always hope!" When his days in this world are done, he can always rely on the strength and power of the True Tzaddik to argue his case before the Heavenly Court. And he knows that in the end, the True Tzaddik—Rebbe Nachman—will help to cleanse and rectify his soul.

WHAT DOES THIS MEAN TO ME?

So there is a Tzaddik who is very great and has wellsprings of teachings and advice to offer. How can I benefit from this Tzaddik? What does being attached to this Tzaddik mean to me on a personal level?

First of all, just knowing about such a Tzaddik is of great benefit. Everyone who is in a position of responsibility knows the importance of having someone to depend on in all situations. This very great Tzaddik is available to everyone, offering advice and counsel in all times of need. On a personal level, one's burden is somewhat lighter.

A person who is attached to such a Tzaddik gains so much more. When we recall the days of Moses or King David, we envision the glory days of the Jewish nation. This is because these great Tzaddikim, if they are not hindered by opposition, bring out the best in each person and enhance the individual's pride in himself and what he can accomplish (see *Likutey Moharan* 17:1). These Tzaddikim know each person's "pressure points" and which buttons to push in order to get the person on the express train to success. (One of Rebbe Nachman's major themes is how to recognize one's greatness and capabilities, yet remain humble.) Everyone can accomplish great things, but the true leader is the one who understands each individual and can match the best advice in Torah with that person's unique needs.

In order to find the True Tzaddik, the one who will best lead you on your spiritual path, you must search for him. Just as you would pursue the perfect mate, hunt for a top job, or search out the right home, so too, you must expend great effort to find your true leader. This might mean searching and seeking, again and again, for the spiritual teachings that quench the thirst of your soul.

Additionally, you should pray to God to direct you to the truth, to find the True Tzaddik. The means for seeking the Tzaddik are limited by one's knowledge. Whatever you understand of spirituality will guide you to what you think is right. Yet prayer can bring you to a higher level. It can elevate you far above your capabilities and enable you to find the True Tzaddik.

THE
TOOLS

HERE WE DISCUSS the basic tools that every Jew needs to become the best person he can be. They are: Torah, prayer, doing *mitzvot* and giving charity.

TORAH refers to the Torah that God gave us at Mount Sinai. This Torah includes both the Written Law (Bible) and the Oral Law (the Talmud and holy writings derived from Talmudic teachings, as well as the Kabbalah).

PRAYER refers to our ability to communicate with God; to plead, beg and cajole Him to answer our pleas and requests; and to otherwise bond with God.

MITZVOT are the laws of the Torah that we are commanded to perform.

CHARITY is an outstanding example of what the *mitzvot* allow us to attain.

These ideas are the "tools" with which we can connect to God and communicate with Him, even though He seems abstract in today's world. With these tools, we can readily find God and realize how close He is to us, and have a meaningful relationship with Him.

18

TORAH

Torah is greater than everything and includes every-thing. It is even greater than prophecy (Tzaddik #421).

OVER 3,300 YEARS AGO God gave the Torah to the Jewish people at Mount Sinai. The Revelation at Sinai was a watershed event in human history, being the first and only time that God revealed Himself to an entire nation of millions of men, women and children. The Jewish people, newly released from slavery in Egypt, responded by committing themselves to following God and His Laws, which were encapsulated in a work known as the Torah. This work comprises both the Written Law (the Bible) and the Oral Law (the Talmud and other holy writings derived from Talmudic teachings, as well as the Kabbalah).

The Torah is more than a book of laws—it is the blueprint for the creation of the world. The Midrash states, "God looked into the Torah and created the world" (*Bereishit Rabbah* 1:1)—meaning that all the moral under-pinnings of the world are based on the Torah. It's not that God created parents and then told us to honor them;

God created parents *because* we should honor them! God didn't create poor people and then tell us to give charity; He created poor people *because* we have a mandate to give charity. The *mitzvot* (commandments) are actually gateways to God, each one a tiny sliver of light revealing God's Infinite Wisdom.

Just as the Torah is intimately connected with the creation of the world, it is closely tied to humanity itself. The Talmud notes that the Torah contains 613 *mitzvot*. There are 248 positive commandments, paralleling the bones and organs of the human body, and 365 prohibitive commandments, corresponding to the number of days in a year (*Makkot* 23b). The *Zohar* (I, 170b) takes this a step further, stating that the 365 prohibitive commandments parallel the number of veins and sinews in the human body. Therefore the verse states, "This is the Torah, man…" (Numbers 19:14), because the human being was formed to correspond to the Torah in every way!*

The implications are twofold. First, it means that each of us can connect with Torah in any number of ways, since each part of us represents one part of Torah or another. Second, it helps us realize that even our mundane existence is a stepping stone to spiritual living and spiritual growth.

The way to acquire Torah is through study. The Torah is not a book of knowledge that one reads in order to absorb its contents. It is a spiritual light filled with Godly energy, embodying the wisdom that God imparted to us so we can get to know Him. We must apply ourselves to Torah study to understand its simple meaning, as well as try to immerse ourselves in its deeper waters of allusions

---

* See *Anatomy of the Soul*, published by the Breslov Research Institute.

and mystical teachings. As Maimonides writes, "Torah will remain only with one who exerts himself for it!" (*RaMBaM, Yad HaChazakah, Hilkhot Talmud Torah* 3:12).

The quantity of material that a person studies is not as important as the effort he puts into it. While a seasoned scholar will naturally be able to cover many pages of Torah and Talmud, the more modest goals of the beginning Torah student are just as precious to God. The important thing is to make a daily study schedule and stick to it, rain or shine. Over the course of weeks and months, you will begin to see every small "deposit" adding up to a sizable investment.

Torah study is absolutely and unquestionably great. In fact, "It is your life" (Deuteronomy 30:20). Were this not so, we wouldn't face so many obstacles while trying to acquire this valuable commodity. Anyone who wishes to enter the wondrous and majestic world of Torah must be prepared to overcome many barriers that stand between him and a true understanding of Torah.

Someone once asked Rebbe Nachman's advice about a certain devotion in serving God. The Rebbe told him to study Torah. When the man objected, "But I do not know how to learn!" the Rebbe answered, "Pray! With prayer, everything becomes possible. The greatest good can be achieved through prayer" (*Likutey Moharan* II, 111).

Rebbe Nachman set the bar very high for his followers. He recommended that they study enough each day so that at the end of the year they would have completed: 1) the entire Talmud with the commentaries of *Rashi, Tosafot, Rif* and *Rabbeinu Asher*, 2) the entire *Shulchan Arukh* (Code of Jewish Law), 3) all the Midrashim, 4) the holy *Zohar*, and 5) the writings of the ARI (see *Rabbi*

Nachman's Wisdom #76). This study schedule amounts to some 20,000 pages annually!

But after listing his ideal study schedule, Rebbe Nachman told his followers not to be anxious if they found themselves incapable of completing everything he suggested. "One can be a religious Jew even if he can't study that much," the Rebbe assured them. "Even without being a scholar, he can still be a Tzaddik. Deep perception cannot be attained without Talmudic and *halakhic* scholarship, but even the simplest Jew can be righteous and a Tzaddik."

WHAT DOES THIS MEAN TO ME ?

Learning Torah is a lifetime job. Even great scholars who have mastered many pages of Torah continually discover new insights the more they study. Try to set reasonable goals for yourself and begin to master the material on a daily schedule that works for you, not one that is overly burdened so that you have to give it up a while later.

The Midrash speaks about a person who looks at the vastness of Torah and says, "Who can learn all this? Thirty chapters of *Nezikin*, thirty chapters of *Keilim*, twenty-four chapters of *Shabbat*..." But the wise man studies two laws today and two laws tomorrow, and so on until he learns it all (*Vayikra Rabbah* 19:2).

Don't get frightened or discouraged by how much there is to learn. By studying a set amount each day and never letting a day pass without studying, you will gradually accumulate more and more Torah knowledge.

Even if you forget what you've studied, don't despair. Our Sages say that in the World to Come, everyone will remember whatever they learned. View yourself as the day-laborer who is paid to pour water into barrels that are full of holes. The foolish man says, "Why waste my time?" But the wise man says, "I'm being paid by the day. What difference does it make to me if the barrels fill up or not? They're paying me to pour water." So too, the person who studies Torah is rewarded for the time he spends studying, not for what he remembers (*Rabbi Nachman's Wisdom* #26; see *Vayikra Rabbah* 19:2).

Whether you're taking your first steps in Torah study or are already familiar with the importance of this mitzvah, Rebbe Nachman offers these guidelines for success:

PRAY. Ask God to allow you the privilege of studying Torah, and plead with Him to help you understand what you study. As Rebbe Nachman teaches: One must cry and pray very hard to get to understand Torah (*Likutey Moharan* I, 21:8).

The Rebbe himself did this. When he began to study Mishnah, he found it very difficult to understand. He wept and cried before God until he was able to comprehend it by himself. Later, when he began studying the Talmud, the same thing happened. Again he cried bitterly until he was worthy of understanding. This was true even of esoteric studies such as the *Zohar* and the writings of the ARI. Understanding came only after he had prayed, pleaded and cried (*Rabbi Nachman's Wisdom, His Praises* #8).

BE DILIGENT AND DETERMINED. It's not enough to buy the books and display them on your bookshelf.

Diligence and devotion to the task are absolutely essential. One of the most important keys to diligence is the setting of realistic goals. It's good to have short-term goals and long-term goals, but above all, they need to be doable. Aiming for what is possible builds enthusiasm; reaching for the impossible destroys it.

Even with commitment and devotion, there are times when your daily goals cannot be met. On certain days, like Yom Kippur and Purim, when everyone is busy with prayer and the *mitzvot* of the day, it becomes impossible to carry a full load of learning. The same is true for the out-of-the-ordinary days when you've got to travel somewhere, or marry off a child and the like. In such cases, the best thing to do is what Reb Noson himself did. Reb Noson designed different study plans for different days. For example, the amount of Codes he would undertake to study would depend on what that day's schedule would allow—so much for a weekday, so much for a Friday, so much for a Shabbat or festival, so much for a day of travel. Each day had different hours available for Torah study—some days more, some days less; the amount was not his main concern. What was most important for Reb Noson—and what is most important for us—was keeping to the goals he himself established and committed himself to fulfill (*Rabbi Eliyahu Chaim Rosen*).

AIM FOR BROAD KNOWLEDGE. Rebbe Nachman emphasized the need for a general and extensive knowledge of Torah. Accordingly, the Rebbe favored the study method that produces broad knowledge, rather than the approach that develops analytical prowess. Spending months on dissecting a page or two of Talmud may turn a person into a sort of "specialist" and sharpen his faculty for dialectics, but ultimately it leaves the majority of students ignorant of most Talmudic tractates and, even worse, its laws.

Map out the areas you intend to learn, focusing on covering as much ground as time will allow. This way, you will have little trouble finishing each book you begin and have enough time to review it, too, thereby gaining a broad knowledge of Torah. Rebbe Nachman compared this kind of study to a world traveler for whom each destination is a feather in his cap. At the end of his life, when he reaches the World to Come, the Torah student will be able to boast about his many "travels" and "journeys," just like all the jet-setters who are always talking about the exotic places they've visited. By studying all the books of Torah, you will be able to say, "I was in this book, I spent time in that set of writings..." (*Rabbi Nachman's Wisdom* #28).

UNDERSTAND AND ENUNCIATE. Rebbe Nachman suggests that you study rapidly—with speed and simplicity—and not spend too much time on each detail. Try to understand each thing in its own context and enunciate the words of Torah as you study them. There is no need to elucidate the words as you progress down the page; if you just carry on, the meaning will become clear as you proceed (ibid., #76). It is good, however, for a person to elucidate his studies in the language he understands (*Likutey Moharan* I, 118). Either way, you must work to understand the material you're studying. It's not enough to just repeat the words without knowing what you're saying. Lack of understanding cannot be considered learning (*Sichot v'Sippurim*, p. 87, #13).

KEEP GOING. What happens when you're trying to decipher the simple meaning of the text and you still don't understand? From Rebbe Nachman's advice, it's clear that the thing to do is to keep going. If, while studying, you come to a sentence or two that you don't understand, or some concept that is beyond your comprehension, don't stop there. Most texts, after all, have difficult passages. Just mark the unclear point and proceed further. This way, your quick study will enable you to absorb a lot. You will be able to review what you have studied for a second and a third time. And because you will have studied so much more since you last attempted to comprehend this material, you will succeed in understanding it the next time around. Even if there are some things you never understand, the quantity outweighs all else (*Rabbi Nachman's Wisdom* #76).

The method of study that the Rebbe advises is actually mentioned in the Talmud and in later works (*Avodah Zarah* 19a; *Orchot Tzaddikim* #27; *ShLaH, Shavuot*; *Maharal* in *Netivot Olam, Netiv HaTorah*; and many other leading Codifiers).

When Rebbe Nachman told Reb Noson to study Kabbalah, Reb Noson complained that there were many points in the *Etz Chaim* (the ARI's main treatise in Kabbalah) that he did not understand. The Rebbe advised him to mark off each part he failed to comprehend. "The next time you study it, you will understand it, and then you can erase the mark." Afterwards Reb Noson said that each time he reviewed the *Etz Chaim*, the marks became fewer and fewer (*Rabbi Eliyahu Chaim Rosen*).

GUARD YOUR TONGUE. Rebbe Nachman teaches: Every Jew is a letter in the Torah. Thus, there are 600,000 letters in the Torah, equivalent to the 600,000 Jewish souls in Creation (see *Zohar Chadash, Shir HaShirim* 91a). When you find fault in a fellow Jew, you are, as it were, finding a blemish in the Torah and rendering it incomplete. But when you refrain from speaking against or belittling another Jew, and emphasize the other's good points, you will also find the Torah perfectly beautiful. You will then have a deep love for the Torah, and this love will lead you to great diligence in your studies (*Rabbi Nachman's Wisdom* #91).

19

PRAYER

Rebbe Nachman teaches: A Jew's main attachment to God is through prayer (Likutey Moharan II, 84). Through his prayers, each Jew acquires absolute mastery and control—he can achieve whatever he desires (ibid., I, 97).

PRAYER IS PERHAPS the most potent tool God gave man to shape his world. We often feel we are "victims of circumstance," that God is in control and we must do whatever He wants unwillingly. Rebbe Nachman states emphatically that this is not the case. We have tremendous power to change our lives and the lives of everyone around us for the better...through prayer.

Prayer is not just reciting the printed words of the *siddur* (Jewish prayer book). It is all about developing a relationship with God. Our Sages call prayer *avodat ha-lev*, "service of the heart." Real prayer happens when we look deep into ourselves to see what we need, and reach out to God, the only One who can make it happen. Prayer enables us to speak to God; to plead, beg and cajole Him to answer our pleas and requests; and to otherwise bond with God.

The formal prayers that Jews recite morning, afternoon and evening were composed more than 2,000 years ago by the Men of the Great Assembly, a group of Sages led by Ezra the Scribe. While these prayers are mandatory for all Jews, variations in *nusach*, or style of the prayer service, subsequently evolved among different Jewish communities. Thus, *Nusach Ashkenaz* refers to the order of the prayers and the special melodies sung during synagogue services by Jews whose families originated in Central and Eastern Europe. *Nusach Sefard* and *Nusach Ha'ARI* are followed by Chassidic Jews. *Nusach Eidot HaMizrach* is followed by Iraqi Jews and others who abide by the *halakhic* opinions of the Ben Ish Chai. *Nusach Teiman* is followed by Yemenite Jews, and *Minhag Bnei Roma* is followed by Italian Jews.

In addition to the formal prayers, prayers may be said at any time of day and in one's mother tongue. The prayers that a person composes himself are often the most meaningful to him. In this regard, Rebbe Nachman encouraged his followers to engage in *hitbodedut*, or private prayer, setting a time and place to speak to God every day. Reb Noson writes how Rebbe Nachman first introduced him to *hitbodedut*: "Rebbe Nachman put his arm around my shoulder and said, 'It's also good to talk your heart out to God as you would to a true, good friend.'" A daily session of *hitbodedut* can go far to help a person establish a real connection with God.

Rebbe Nachman teaches that prayer has the power to change nature (*Likutey Moharan* I, 30:8; I, 216). This applies both to the forces of nature and to human nature. Reb Noson once said, "Nothing can help a person break his unwanted desires except prayer. The reason for this is quite simple. Normally, someone who breaks his desires is left with two desires, just as when a person breaks something in half and is left with two pieces." But with prayer, we are able to rid ourselves completely of all our unwanted desires (cf. *Siach Sarfey Kodesh* 1-511).

Prayer can even go so far as to nullify Heavenly decrees before—and even after—they are issued (*The Aleph-Bet Book*, Prayer A:14). Reb Shimon, one of Rebbe Nachman's closest followers, experienced this personally. When his infant son fell deathly ill, Reb Shimon asked the Rebbe to pray for the child's recovery. But Rebbe Nachman did not respond. Forlorn and without hope, Reb Shimon returned home. His wife understood well the implication of the Rebbe's silence. But instead of despairing, she spent that entire night sitting by the infant's crib and praying for her child. The next morning, Rebbe Nachman saw Reb Shimon and ran towards him with great joy, saying, "Look at the great power of prayer! Last night, the decree was sealed. The infant's death was imminent. And now, not only has the decree been nullified, but Heaven has granted him long life as well!" Tradition has it that Reb Shimon's son lived close to one hundred years (*Aveneha Barzel*, p. 39, #60).

WHAT DOES THIS MEAN TO ME ?

Having the power to connect to God on a daily and even hourly basis brings a tremendous sense of self-importance to your life. God is waiting to hear from you! God cares! But how can you know this? Perseverance. Each time you turn to God, you are connecting with Him. As you become more proficient in pouring out your heart, you will feel a certain feeling of closeness. Sometimes, though, it doesn't seem to work. You sit listless, without emotion. Don't despair. Just persevere. You will see the answers to your prayers.

Our Sages teach, "A person's prayers are not answered unless he places his very soul into it" (*Ta'anit* 8a). Rashi elaborates, "He is entirely focused, with full concentration." Someone once asked me about this. "I pray and pray, but I don't see the unhealthy getting better, I don't see the improvements," he told me. I said to him, "When was the last time (or maybe the first time) that you prayed as if your life completely depended on it?!" It's one thing to offer lip service, but another to really mean it. From my personal viewpoint, I know that prayers are answered. Not always do we do it right, but if we keep at it, it works! (cf. *Likutey Moharan* I, 223).

There are many opportunities to pray throughout the day. Here are different types of prayer that can help you forge a connection with God:

REGULAR DAILY PRAYERS. The three daily prayer services are known as *Shacharit* (the morning prayer), *Minchah* (the afternoon prayer) and *Ma'ariv* (the evening prayer). On Shabbat and Jewish festivals, an additional service called *Musaf* is recited after *Shacharit*, and on Yom Kippur a fifth service, *Ne'ilah*, is said after *Minchah*. Composed as they were by Sages who had *ruach ha-kodesh* (Divine inspiration), they have become the standard prayers for all Jewish communities in the format of the *siddur*, which varies slightly from community to community.

The fact that the prayers are written in Hebrew could stop people from using an incredibly powerful tool. Knowing what you're saying certainly makes the task easier. But there are many advantages to praying in the original Hebrew—among them the fact that the words were chosen for their Divine inspiration, and were written by holy people who knew the power of prayer. Therefore it seems most advisable to pray from a Hebrew/English *siddur*, so that any time you don't fully understand the original, you can look at the translation and appreciate the meaning of what you're saying. If it's too difficult, then the *halakhah* clearly states that one should pray in the language he is familiar with.

Whenever you can, pray with a minyan (quorum of ten men). The Talmud states, "The prayers of the individual may be rejected, but the prayers of the many are never rejected" (*Ta'anit* 8a). Pray with joy and happiness, even to the point of clapping your hands and singing the words. As Rebbe Nachman said, "I put great value in the Baal Shem Tov's way of praying—with exertion and joy" (*Tovot Zikhronot* #5). However, one should not pray in a manner that disturbs others, nor use mannerisms designed to draw attention to himself. Better to pray simply, with as much concentration as you can muster.

The Rebbe never asked his followers to give up their family's *nusach*, or style of formal prayer, which is "inherited" from father to son. It makes no difference which *nusach* one follows—*Sefardi, Mizrachi, Ashkenazi,* Chassidic or some other. Rebbe Nachman said: Chassidut has nothing to do with *nusach*. One can be a Chassid and still pray *Nusach Ashkenaz* (*Siach Sarfey Kodesh* I-90).

HITBODEDUT. One of Rebbe Nachman's most important and best-known teachings introduces the idea of private, secluded prayer as the ultimate level in our relationship with God. Unlike the regular daily prayers, *hitbodedut* is prayer in one's mother tongue and in one's own words. It is a "one on one" audience with God, an opportunity to release all our inner feelings—the joys and depressions, the successes and frustrations—that we experience each day. Through *hitbodedut*, we examine and re-examine our actions and motives, correcting the flaws and errors of the past while seeking the proper path for the future.

Hitbodedut can be done anywhere, as long as it's quiet and private. A private room is good, a park better, out in the fields or forests still better. During *hitbodedut*, you'll talk to God about all the things you're going through. Tell Him the various pressures you are under, your personal situation and that of others in your family, and also of the Jewish people as a whole. *Hitbodedut* is also a time for self-judgment, to review what you've done and what mistakes you'd like to amend. And don't forget the mundane side of life. Pray that you get the right clothing back from the dry cleaners, and that you don't overpay on an item you plan to purchase. Nothing is too trivial to discuss with God. As long as you even think you need it, pray for it!

Certainly, a person must focus his prayers on the ultimate goal: serving God. Pray, plead, ask and beseech God that He reveal His ways to you, that He show you His mercy, that you merit to come closer to Him. Pray that you will be able to perform His will, each mitzvah in its own time. Pray to experience the beauty of Torah and the sweetness of the *mitzvot.**

Reb Nachman Chazan once labored tirelessly to erect Reb Noson's sukkah. That evening, while sitting in the sukkah, Reb Nachman remarked, "There is a different feeling of joy and satisfaction when sitting in a sukkah that one has worked very hard to build." Reb Noson replied, "That may be, but this you haven't yet tried. Spend an entire day crying out to God, 'Master of the Universe! Let me taste the true taste of sukkah!' Then see what feelings a person can experience in the sukkah!" (*Aveneha Barzel*, p. 52, #12).

PSALMS. This treasury of 150 songs of praise, or Psalms, expresses the full spectrum of highs and lows in the turbulent life of King David, along with his unceasing reliance on and praise of God. Because the emotions David describes are so universal, his Psalms have become the companion of Jews in all times and situations. Whatever you're going through, you'll find a Psalm to match—and you'll also find beautiful Psalms of thanksgiving to express your gratitude to God when things are going great.

TIKKUN HAKLALI (THE GENERAL REMEDY). In a most original teaching, Rebbe Nachman identified ten specific chapters of Psalms that have the power to rectify every sin at its root. This is the *Tikkun HaKlali*, or General Remedy. Each sin, explains the Rebbe, has its own rectification. To repair the spiritual damage caused by a particular sin, we must apply the particular remedy appropriate for that sin.

---

* For an excellent "how-to" book about *hitbodedut*, see *Where Earth and Heaven Kiss: A Guide to Rebbe Nachman's Path of Meditation* by Ozer Bergman, published by the Breslov Research Institute.

Yet the task of tackling each sin one by one is far too big for most people to undertake. If only there was a single rectification that would zap all sins simultaneously! There is. Rebbe Nachman's General Remedy counteracts the spiritual damage caused by wasted seed in particular and all other sins in general. It consists of the saying of these Ten Psalms: 16, 32, 41, 42, 59, 77, 90, 105, 137, 150.

The Rebbe referenced the Ten Psalms in an unprecedented vow that continues to bring hundreds of thousands of people to pray at his grave in Uman more than 200 years after his passing. In the presence of two witnesses, the Rebbe declared, "Whoever comes to my gravesite, recites the *Tikkun HaKlali* and donates something to charity for my sake, I promise that I will intercede on his behalf. No matter how terrible his sins, I will do everything in my power to remove that person from Gehinnom!" (*Rabbi Nachman's Wisdom* #141). This is a most incredible promise, one that no other Tzaddik ever issued. Consider the power of this promise. By virtue of traveling to Rebbe Nachman's gravesite, reciting the *Tikkun HaKlali* and giving charity, a person earns himself the services of a most powerful and eloquent defense lawyer who will argue his case before the Heavenly Tribunal on his Day of Judgment!

The *Tikkun HaKlali* can be said anywhere, not just at the Rebbe's gravesite but wherever you happen to be: in synagogue, in your home, in a park, on an airplane, or even in Disney World! It takes but a few minutes, but it serves to remind us that we have to connect with our Maker, we cannot expect to live without responsibility, and we must display the desire to make amends at any and all times. It's a perfect remedy, giving everyone a means to return to his Source.*

TIKKUN CHATZOT (THE MIDNIGHT LAMENT). Every night around midnight, Breslover Chassidim traditionally rise from their sleep and mourn the destruction of the Temple in a prayer called *Tikkun Chatzot* (the Midnight Lament). Midnight is considered a time of Divine favor and this prayer, which expresses grief over the loss of the Temple, also conveys yearning for the Final Redemption and the rebuilding of the Temple. *Tikkun Chatzot* is not a mandatory prayer, but a "labor of love" by those who truly yearn to know God and who feel pain and anguish over His concealment in this world.

The midnight prayer consists of two parts. *Tikkun Rachel* contains Psalms and laments about the destruction of the Temple and the catastrophes that have befallen the Jewish people in exile. *Tikkun Leah* includes Psalms and other holy writings expressing praise and yearning for God and His Redemption.

Being distant from God is like being asleep: the deeper the sleep, the harder it is to be aroused to serve God. Furthermore, sleep is compared to "lesser" wisdom, an unconscious existence, while awakening corresponds to awareness. Thus, rising for *Tikkun Chatzot* "breaks" sleep and eliminates the distance between us and God (*Likutey Halakhot, Hashkamat HaBoker* 1:12). It helps us break our spiritual slumber and recognize the need to become more aware of our surroundings and the situations in which we find

* For more insights and the complete text of the *Tikkun HaKlali*, see *Rabbi Nachman's Tikkun*, published by the Breslov Research Institute.

ourselves. It is also analogous to finding the good points in ourselves amid the "darkness" all around (see Chapter 11, What are the Good Points?).*

Rebbe Nachman suggests that when reciting *Tikkun Chatzot* and similar prayers, one should apply the verses to himself (*Likutey Moharan* II, 101). Because it is a most heartrending expression of suffering and anguish, *Tikkun Chatzot* is a perfect vehicle for releasing one's own pent-up feelings. After Rebbe Nachman passed away, Reb Noson found it impossible to express his agony over his loss. Only when reciting the *Tikkun Chatzot* was he able to find consolation (*Rabbi Eliyahu Chaim Rosen*).

LIKUTEY TEFILOT. Many times we pray, but we don't "feel" it. We are distant from the prayers, or perhaps we don't find the way we feel expressed in their words. In this regard, many optional prayers were written by many of the greatest Jewish scholars. These can be found in *Sha'arey Tzion*, *Taktu Tefilot* and similar works. Rebbe Nachman greatly valued these optional prayers and recited them many times himself (*Rabbi Nachman's Wisdom, His Praises* #10).

Rebbe Nachman taught Reb Noson the idea of "turning Torah into prayers" (*Likutey Moharan* II, 25). In other words, whenever you hear or study words of Torah, you should make a prayer out of it. When you're studying the laws of *tefilin*, *tzitzit*, Shabbat, Pesach, *lulav*, *shofar*, *matzah*, and so on, translate them into prayers beseeching God to help you fulfill the mitzvah

---

* For an in-depth look at the *Tikkun Chatzot* and the prayer itself in both Hebrew and English, see *The Sweetest Hour* by Avraham Greenbaum, published by the Breslov Research Institute.

to the best of your ability and with a wealth of joy and happiness.

Reb Noson took this advice to heart and composed his own book of prayers called *Likutey Tefilot* (Collected Prayers), which he based on Rebbe Nachman's Torah teachings in *Likutey Moharan*. *Likutey Tefilot* is a collection of over 200 magnificent prayers on all topics and circumstances in life. Each is infused with Reb Noson's great longing and holy desire to connect with God. Many men and women recite these prayers as their own, using Reb Noson's heartfelt words and humble sincerity to reach out to God.*

---

* *Likutey Tefilot* is presently being translated into English as *The Fiftieth Gate*. Four volumes of the projected seven-volume series have been published by the Breslov Research Institute. Selected prayers from *Likutey Tefilot* have also been adapted and compiled in a special prayer book for women, *Between me & You: Heartfelt prayers for each Jewish woman*, by Yitzchok Leib Bell (Nachas Books, 2012).

20

MITZVOT

Observe the commandments, statutes and laws that I am commanding you today, to do them (Deuteronomy 7:11).

"Today, to do them"—and tomorrow [in the World to Come], to receive the reward for doing them (Rashi).

Reb Noson writes: Whatever service a person performs in devotion to God makes him a lender to God! This is because, "There is no reward [great enough] for mitzvot in This World" (Kiddushin 39b). Therefore, when a person performs mitzvot, God is obligated to pay him his reward in the Future World. Until God pays him, he is considered a lender to God (Likutey Halakhot, Shabbat 6:9).

THE COMMANDMENTS, OR *MITZVOT*, are the laws that God gave us in the Torah. There are 248 positive commandments and 365 prohibitive commandments, for a total of 613. The *mitzvot* are God's directives on how to live right, take hold of our actions, and focus on the true goal: getting close to God. They are not man-made counsel or recommendations, but laws designed by God to help each person mold and form himself into the best person he can be.

The Hebrew word *mitZVah* (מצוה) comes from the root word *le-tZaVet* (לצוות), which means "to join." This teaches us that the performance of *mitzvot* is the means by which we can "join" and attach ourselves to God in order to experience the Divine.

We often hear people say, "I can't get my act together" or, "I feel like I'm all over the place." This is because through sin, we disperse the sparks of our souls and become spread out, making it difficult to pull things together. When we perform *mitzvot*, we are actually collecting the dispersed sparks of our souls and becoming whole again. Reb Noson adds that each mitzvah, in one way or another, must be performed with a material item. The objective of doing *mitzvot* is to take the physical item and elevate it to the spiritual realm, using that corporeal item to join and connect with God (cf. *Likutey Halakhot, Netilat Yadayim LiSeudah* 6:64).

Rebbe Nachman has a most unusual approach to the idea of connecting to God through the *mitzvot*. He explains:

> The *mitzvot* express the wisdom of God, which is why all the commandments have different measures and specifications. For example, why is the prescription of a particular mitzvah as it is? Because that is what the wisdom of God requires. The same is true of the prescription of a different mitzvah; it is in accordance with the wisdom of God (*Likutey Moharan* I, 30:3).

In his discussion, Rebbe Nachman teaches that there are awesome levels of Perceptions of Godliness. By performing the *mitzvot*, we connect with God's wisdom, which allows us to attain deep Perceptions of Godliness. Through *mitzvot*, we can attain great and awesome spiritual levels. The Rebbe compares human perception with the pupil of the eye. The pupil includes within it all the large things that stand opposite it. Take, for example, a large mountain. When it stands opposite the pupil, the entire mountain is contained within the pupil that sees it. In a similar fashion, through our performance of *mitzvot*, we can attain perceptions of Godliness that are normally beyond our ken.

The *mitzvot* cover all areas in life, providing a sort of "cradle to grave" management for living. The positive *mitzvot* include observing Shabbat and Jewish festivals, eating kosher food, praying, studying Torah, being honest in business, giving charity, doing acts of kindness, and so on. The prohibitive commandments include abstaining from immoral behavior, refraining from slander, profanity, flattery and all other types of improper speech, avoiding falsehood, stealing and other financial transgressions, and more. Each mitzvah has within it many categories that are also considered *mitzvot*. For example, under the mitzvah of doing acts of kindness, one can visit the sick, provide financial help to someone struggling with debts, offer comforting words to someone who is beset with troubles, or even just smile at a person who looks a little down. Each act of kindness is a mitzvah unto itself!

WHAT DOES THIS MEAN TO ME ?

When it comes to doing *mitzvot*, you may find yourself in a quandary. On the one hand, you see many religious Jews keeping the *mitzvot*. On the other hand, you hear other Jews saying, "Why keep *mitzvot*? Isn't it enough to be a good person? Besides, isn't every good deed I do a *mitzvah*?"

As mentioned above, the *mitzvot* are not man-made. God, Who created each one of us, designed the *mitzvot* to fulfill the essential needs of our souls. When a person performs a mitzvah, he strengthens a certain part of his soul. The *mitzvot* that are detailed in the Torah and the *Shulchan Arukh*, and rabbinically-mandated *mitzvot*, are also channels that open up the Perceptions of Godliness to us. We can just glide through life thinking we have a connection to God. But do we really? Do we really feel attached to Him? The *mitzvot* are the "Velcro" that fastens us to God.

Interestingly, it's not just the *doing* of the *mitzvot* that's important, but the *thoughts* and *intentions* that the person has that empower each mitzvah. If you toss a coin into a beggar's cup without thinking, your mitzvah is much less complete than if you give charity with the intention of fulfilling one of God's commandments.

In answer to the second question: Yes, good deeds are important and make the world a much nicer place to live. But a good deed to one person doesn't mean the same thing to another. You might think that holding the door open for an old lady is a great kindness. But that old lady's daughter knows that if her mother doesn't exercise her muscles and open the door for herself, she will become frailer and weaker. A good deed is subject to interpretation; a mitzvah always has the same specifications and parameters, no matter who performs it.

Reb Noson once remarked about the amount of *mitzvot* we were given. He said, "When a person likes someone, does he give him a heavy burden or a light burden? Why did God give us what seems to be a heavy burden of 613 *mitzvot*? But if there were only a few *mitzvot*, then only those who were in that specific situation would be able to perform them. For example, the wealthy would give charity, the brilliant scholars would study Torah, farmers would obey the agricultural laws, and so on. However, with so many *mitzvot*, there is always some mitzvah that any person can perform" (*Rabbi Eliyahu Chaim Rosen*).

Like anything good or worthwhile, doing *mitzvot* often comes at a price. Some *mitzvot* are costly—a good pair of *tefilin* can cost upwards of $1,000, and Shabbat and festival meals (especially Pesach expenses) add up. Having to stop work early on Fridays in the winter can be an inconvenience and even a deal-breaker when you're in the middle of a lucrative business transaction. Not driving to synagogue on Shabbat when you live a couple of miles away can mean a healthy walk in the summer, but a bitterly cold trek in the winter. Our Sages assure us, "According to the effort is the reward" (*Avot* 5:23). The harder it is for us, the more we gain in the end.

Rebbe Nachman teaches that each mitzvah a person performs creates a candle. That candle will be used by the person in the future to "search the King's treasury"—that is, to choose his rewards in the World to Come (*Likutey Moharan* I, 275). The more *mitzvot* we do, the greater number of candles we create with which to search God's treasury, and the more rewards (after all, God owes us!) we will receive for doing *mitzvot*.

The main thing, Rebbe Nachman emphasizes, is the joy we feel when doing *mitzvot*. Sitting down to enjoy a Shabbat meal, praying with fervor and a feeling of connection to God, studying and understanding a difficult passage of Torah, helping another person—each mitzvah is an entire construct unto itself. When we are happy with our devotions we fill these constructs with joy—and they, in turn, fill us with joy! (see *Likutey Moharan* I, 178).

21
CHARITY

Charity is equal to all the other mitzvot combined (*The Aleph-Bet Book*, Charity A:14).

IN THE PREVIOUS CHAPTER we spoke about performing *mitzvot* and mentioned charity. The greatness of charity cannot be overstated; there are very few *mitzvot* that are as powerful as charity to draw all kinds of blessing to ourselves and the world at large. Our charitable deeds and acts of kindness "force" God, as it were, to act towards us with kindness. Thus, our charitable acts open the gates of Heaven and allow for even greater bounty to flow down to us (see *Likutey Moharan* II, 4:1-3).

Ostensibly, it may look like charity means taking money out of our pockets and putting it in someone else's. But the reverse is really the case. The giver benefits far more than the receiver—even to the point of getting money back in return! It is written, "Bring all your tithes to the treasury... 'Please, test me with this,' says God, '[and see] if I do not open the floodgates of Heaven and pour down upon you blessings without end'" (Malakhi 3:10). Commenting on this verse, the Talmud teaches that although we are prohibited from challenging God, we are actually permitted to test God to see if giving tithes brings us blessing (*Ta'anit* 9a). In other words, if we earn $10,000 and tithe it, we can expect God to replenish that ten percent—and even more. When we tithe our income, we can expect an increase in our income!

The power of charity is awesome. Charity has the power to open the closed doors of employment and business opportunities (*Likutey Moharan* II, 4:2-3), promote peace in one's home, and bring healing (ibid., I, 57:8; II, 3). It also helps a person distinguish between reality and illusion (ibid., I, 25:4) and elevates him to the level where all his prayers are answered (ibid., I, 2:1-4).

Charity brings peace, as our Sages state, "The more charity, the more peace" (*Avot* 2:7). Rebbe Nachman explains that charity creates a tranquil atmosphere in which people can form satisfactory relationships. In such an atmosphere, words of spirituality can spread and reach those who are very distant from God—not just Jews who are distant from their heritage, but even non-Jews, bringing converts into the fold!

Rebbe Nachman adds that giving charity rectifies many sins. Charity is a rectification for a blemished covenant, for financial wrongdoings (but does not exempt a person from repaying anything taken wrongfully), and for sin in general (*Likutey Moharan* I, 29:9; I, 69:9; I, 115). Charity also allows a person to rise above his animalistic tendencies. It brings him to the level of "Man," and affords him the level of sanctity of the Land of Israel (ibid., I, 37:3-4). Charity helps to reveal Divine Pleasantness and can be beneficial for the raising of one's children (ibid., II, 71).

Charity plays an important role in Breslov thought,

since this practice helps a person focus on the proper path. How? Giving charity is not just something we do with our hands; it also demands the judgmental application of our minds. With charity, we are forced to make decisions: Who is a worthy recipient? Which causes deserve priority? How much should I get involved? Being forced to make decisions teaches us to focus and choose wisely. This naturally spills over into other choices we must make in life—such as everyday living, job opportunities, making major purchases or investments and, of course, spiritual aspirations. Giving charity influences our overall decision-making and focus.

Besides charity, there is a mitzvah of doing *chesed*, acts of kindness. This mitzvah includes hospitality and helping others—the sick, the weak, the bereaved, and so on. In fact, the Talmud teaches that acts of kindness are, in a way, greater than charity (*Sukkah* 49b). If someone doesn't have enough money to contribute to charity, he can still attain all the benefits of giving charity by engaging in acts of kindness.

WHAT DOES THIS MEAN TO ME ?

Are you looking for a daily practice that will make you the decision-maker, channel your contribution so it does the most good, and earn you blessings both in this world and the next? Charity can provide all that, and more.

Like every other mitzvah, charity has specific parameters and requirements for maximum effectiveness. The minimum amount one should give is a tithe, or ten percent of his income. A person may also give fifteen or twenty percent, but no more, lest he become impoverished himself. What if he lacks the means to give ten percent? Someone who is struggling financially should consult with a competent rabbi about what to do and how to give. Some cases, after consultation, will seem not as bad; others will exempt the person until he manages to get back on his feet.

Now you can consider yourself the manager of your funds and distribute them accordingly. Here, too, there are guidelines for making the most impact. Donating your money to any and every cause, no matter how dubious, will not garner the same payback as charity given to worthy causes. Rebbe Nachman teaches that righteous poor people are a good choice, poor Torah scholars or organizations that promote Torah education a better choice. Charity that is given to Tzaddikim is the best choice of all, because giving to them is like giving to many, many Jewish souls (since the Tzaddikim, through their teachings, enable the many to draw close to God) (*Kitzur Likutey Moharan* I, 17:9).*

Giving charity yields many blessings in this world and the next. We've already mentioned some of them above. In Chapter 20 we noted that the performance of *mitzvot* helps to collect and gather in the dispersed and lost sparks of holiness, the sparks of our souls. Giving charity is one of the most potent factors in gathering these sparks. God sends bounty daily to this world, with the intent that His kingship

---

* For a full treatment of the benefits and guidelines of giving charity, see *More Blessed to Give: Rebbe Nachman on Charity*, published by the Breslov Research Institute.

be recognized and elevated. If we do not act accordingly—that is, if we sin—then we cause a shattering of our vessels, we disperse our souls and spread the sparks of holiness throughout the world. Conversely, when we perform *mitzvot*, we gather in those sparks, and gather in the bounty.

When we give charity, not only are we doing a mitzvah, but we are actually taking *our* bounty—that which we chased away due to sin—and placing it in the realm of holiness. This elevates the sparks and even rectifies them. When we give charity, we sustain the realm of holiness. Thus, charity is a most potent force in gathering in the dispersed sparks (*Likutey Moharan* I, 264). And it brings that bounty to us!

Once, when Rabbi Menachem Mendel of Chernobyl heard a lesson of Rebbe Nachman about giving charity, he said, "*Nu!* We have to relearn how to give charity!"

POSITIVE
AND NEGATIVE
TRAITS

REBBE NACHMAN TEACHES THAT the body is called *chomer* (חומר), "matter," while the soul is called *tzurah* (צורה), "form" (see *Likutey Moharan* I, 170). *Chomer*, the body, is actually pliable "raw material" that assumes the "shape" of the soul as it is molded. Someone who seeks a life of materialism will mold his body according to the chosen requirements of that life, and his body will then conceal his spirituality. One who seeks Godliness, on the other hand, will mold and refine his physical nature to be sensitive to the subtlest signals of the soul, so that the soul's innate spirituality will radiate from within.

At the highest levels, the physical body of such a person becomes a spiritual body, similar to that of Moses, whose face "shone" when he descended from Mount Sinai (Exodus 34:29-30, 35); or Adam, whose entire body shone brighter than the noonday sun (*Vayikra Rabbah* 20:2); or the prophet Elijah, who did not die but ascended to Heaven in a "chariot of fire" (see II Kings 2:11).

How can we "shape" our own bodies, controlling our base desires and rising above them? The key is in understanding our strengths and weaknesses, as revealed in our positive and negative traits.

22
THE FOUR ELEMENTS

There are four fundamental elements: fire, air, water and earth. Above, in their transcendent root, they correspond to the four letters of God's Holy Name YHVH (cf. Tikkuney Zohar #22). But below, in our world, they are a mixture of good and bad. The perfect tzaddik, however, has completely distinguished and separated the bad from the good, so that he is without even a residue of bad from any one of these four elements—which encompass all the traits (Likutey Moharan I, 8:5).

FOUR BASIC ELEMENTS make up the material world (these elements should not be confused with the chemical elements). They are:

- Fire—which is hot and dry
- Air—which is hot and damp
- Water—which is cold and damp
- Earth—which is cold and dry

Everything in this world is made up of at least one of the four elements; most possess two or more. The ARI explains that these four elements correspond to the four letters of God's Holy Name *YHVH* (the Tetragrammaton) (*Etz Chaim* 42:3) and also parallel the four levels or realms of physical existence: mineral, vegetable, animal and speaker (i.e., man).

TETRAGRAMMATON	ELEMENT	LEVEL OF EXISTENCE
Apex of *Yod*	Root or single source element	Tzaddik
Yod	Fire	Speaker
Heh	Air	Animal
Vav	Water	Vegetable
Heh	Earth	Mineral

The four elements stem from a single source element. This is alluded to in the verse, "A river flowed out of Eden to water the Garden. From there, it separated into four major rivers" (Genesis 2:10). That is, there is a single source element that divides into four: the four elements. That single source element is the Tzaddik, the righteous person in whose merit the world is sustained. This source element is called the *Yesod HaPashut*, the "simple element," in that at the source, everything is united as one, without differentiation.

It is axiomatic throughout Rebbe Nachman's teachings that *everyone* can become a Tzaddik on a level that is suitable for him. This means that each person can learn to control his physical elements and unify his various attributes. To the extent that a person develops himself spiritually and attains mastery over his body—his four elements—he can merit the title of Tzaddik for his spiritual level. Anyone, at whatever level he may find himself, has the ability to harmonize the four elements within himself and achieve total harmony between his body and soul.

Everything in the world is composed of the four elements, and the continued existence of the world is based on the proper combination and interaction of these elements. Although every person is made up of all four elements, each individual is rooted in a particular letter of the Tetragrammaton and in one element more than the others. Correspondingly, he is also rooted in the specific character trait that derives from that letter and element, as we shall see in the coming chapters. This accounts for the tremendous differences we find in people's temperaments. Some temperaments are rooted in fire (e.g., arrogance and anger), some in air (idle chatter), some in water (sensual gratification) and some in earth (laziness and depression), as will be explained shortly.

* * *

THE FOUR ELEMENTS CONTAIN all the physical resources that a person needs to advance his spiritual growth, but they also contain negative characteristics that can inhibit—and even reverse—that growth. For this reason, the four elements are called "servants." They must serve the soul faithfully in order for a person to ascend in spirituality (cf. *Likutey Moharan* I, 4:12). Reb Noson writes that the three higher elements represent various intellects, while earth, the lowest element, parallels faith, as in, "Dwell in the earth and shepherd faith" (Psalms 37:3) (*Likutey Halakhot, Shechitah* 5:12).

FIRE is the lightest of the four elements in its constitution, as its properties cause heat to rise. On the positive side, it infuses us with energy and zeal to accomplish great things. On the negative side, it burns inside us with passion and turbulence, leading to arrogance (the desire to "rise above" others), anger, jealousy, and the desire for power and honor.

AIR, on its positive side, is life itself; it is our power to breathe and infuse ourselves with freshness and is our vehicle for proper speech and encouraging words. On the negative side, it is the source of idle chatter (the tendency to speak about worthless subjects) and various forms of forbidden speech such as flattery, falsehood, slander, profanity and mockery. Air is also the source of boasting.

WATER brings enjoyment to the entire world, to all levels of mineral, vegetable, animal and human. Therefore water is the root of all sensual pleasure. But from the element of water also come the cravings for all the various lusts. These cravings arouse jealousy and envy, leading to dishonest behavior and outright theft.

EARTH, the lowest and densest of the elements, parallels the attribute of faith. Just as faith can contain the greatest levels despite its being the smallest of the levels, so too, everything we know of "sits" upon the earth and is included in it. Earth represents our physicality, and provides for our free will to rise above the density of our corporeal existence. But it also denotes laziness and depression. A person who is dominated by the material aspects of earth always bemoans his fate and is never satisfied with his lot (Sha'arey Kedushah 1:2).

Interestingly, character traits and attitudes are not among the commandments of the Torah. A whole body of commandments revolves around human relations—for example, to love one's fellow man, to give charity to the poor, to help one's enemy in a fix, not to bear a grudge, not to take revenge, not to hate one's brother in one's heart, and so on. There are also numerous commandments involving man's relationship to God. Nowhere, however, do we find any commandment to be moral, humble, loving, kind, benevolent, compassionate, empathetic or giving. Neither are we commanded not to become angry, not to be arrogant, not to be jealous and not to be spiteful. Even a commandment such as, "Do not hate your brother in your heart" (Leviticus 19:17), can be construed as a behavioral rather than attitudinal directive. If, as we have seen, character traits and attitudes are so essential, why aren't they mentioned in the system of commandments?

The answer is that character traits and attitudes are the goal—and the very basis—of the commandments. Refining and strengthening our moral characteristics is a *precondition* for our successful observance of the commandments. The basic premise of the commandments is that once we act in compliance with the objective morality of the Torah, this morality will become part of our spiritual and emotional makeup. Therefore the Torah does not directly command us "to be," but "to do." For example, acting lovingly towards someone, even if we dislike him, forces us to overcome the attitude we have formed about him that prevents us from seeing him as a fellow human being. Clearly, the goal of the action is an inner transformation. Viewing the commandments as mere behavioral directives misses this crucial point.

We can now see that the system of commandments is designed to help man express, develop and refine his innate character traits. When viewed in this way, the hidden attitudinal directive behind every commandment becomes revealed. The Torah knows that these attitudes and character traits are the basis of the human personality and that they are present, in rudimentary form, from infancy. Perfecting the positive character traits on the one hand, and transmuting the energy of the negative traits on the other hand, presents the most serious challenge we face throughout our lives.

23

EATING AND SLEEPING

Show great compassion for your body. Help it delight in all the spiritual insights and perceptions that the soul perceives.

Your soul is always seeing and comprehending very exalted things. But the body knows nothing of this. Have compassion for the flesh of your body. Purify it. Then the soul will be able to inform it of all that she is always seeing and comprehending (Likutey Moharan I, 22:5).

AS WE HAVE SEEN, fire is the lightest of the four elements and its properties cause heat to rise. Every person has "fire" within himself—it is part and parcel of his digestive tract which, like fire, consumes everything that enters it. Eating is the main source of maintaining this fire. Just as a fire must be fed with fuel in order to keep burning, the digestive tract must be "fed" in order to maintain the person's normal temperature (heat) and function satisfactorily so that the person doesn't fall ill.

But there is eating, and then there is eating. We all know how eating can get out of hand, how one slice of cake or scoop of ice cream can lead to another and another and another. For some people, food has become an all-encompassing passion—witness the fast-food outlets on every corner, snack vending machines in every school, triple-decker hamburgers, jumbo-sized soft drinks, and the worldwide increase in obesity and eating disorders.

Rebbe Nachman calls gluttony a "lust" and lists it ahead of other lusts like sexual desire and avarice (*Likutey Moharan* I, 62:5). Gluttony is the primary lust because Adam, the first man, used it inappropriately. God commanded him one thing—not to eat from the Tree of Knowledge of Good and Evil—but he was overcome by temptation. Ever since, man has been fighting the "battle of the bulge," or counting calories, or indulging in more and different culinary experiences. Indeed, a good part of our day is taken up with food. "What's for breakfast?" "Where should we eat lunch?" "What will we have for dinner?" "What treat should we buy for our coffee break...for our afternoon tea...for a late-night snack?" If you want to understand why so much of our lives is taken up with food, Reb Noson explains simply that the very first sin—the primary lust—was eating, and it is our mission to rectify that sin.

All the laws and customs of eating kosher foods and reciting the blessings on our nourishment are meant to make the ritual of eating a spiritual act. This isn't the only way to elevate our eating. Rebbe Nachman notes that when we eat the special foods prepared for the Shabbat and Jewish festivals, those foods nourish us on a higher plane than weekday eating (cf. *Likutey Moharan* I, 277:4; I, 57:6). Additionally, sparks of holiness are found in most foods. By eating in holiness, we are able to rectify fallen sparks and souls.

Food is digested and absorbed in the bloodstream. When eaten in holiness, it brings to holiness. Otherwise it feeds the body's fire with physicality. When the body is fed with materialistic wants, it succumbs to the evil of the negative traits it possesses. These are the negative characteristics that we all have to battle throughout our lives.

∙ ∙ ∙

SLEEPING, like eating, is an absolute necessity. It allows the body to rest and revitalize itself. It also takes up a lot of our time, rendering those hours spent sleeping as unproductive. Or does it?

Let's understand the meaning of sleep. Sleeping, like eating, is a result of Adam's eating from the Tree. The Talmud teaches that "food leads to sleep" (*Yoma* 18a) and, "Sleep is one-sixtieth of death" (*Berakhot* 57b). Adam's eating from the Tree brought death into the world, which also caused sleep to become a major concern for humanity.

As stated in the previous chapter, earth is the heaviest of the four elements and denotes laziness and depression. A lazy person will spend an inordinate amount of time in bed, and someone who is depressed will sleep a lot. The tendency for extra sleep is symptomatic of an extra dose of the element of earth—of slothfulness, depression, sadness and carelessness. Therefore Rebbe Nachman teaches, "Laziness and depression are the main bite of the Primordial Serpent!" (*Likutey Moharan* I, 189).

The idea of sleep, however, can be misconstrued to mean "wasting" time. In a sense, this is true. Maybe a quarter or even a third of our lives is spent sleeping. But when we rest with the intent of refreshing ourselves so we can pursue our daily activities and devotions, then sleep is actually very productive.

However, human nature has a tendency to seek the "easier" path—the path of rest and recreation. It's easier to fall into laziness and indulge in extra sleep than deal with the pressures of daily living, but the results (and the rewards) will be sorely lacking.

WHAT DOES THIS MEAN TO ME?

In Rebbe Nachman's classic story, "The Lost Princess" (*Rabbi Nachman's Stories* #1), a viceroy spends years searching for a princess. When he finally finds her, he is put to the test to see if he can rescue her. Twice he succumbs to the temptations of eating and sleeping, and only in the end, when he resolves to complete his mission to the nth degree, does he finally succeed.

Reb Noson comments that the first time the viceroy failed is similar to Adam eating from the Tree. The second time parallels the Generation of the Flood, when mankind succumbed to all sorts of immorality and fell into a spiritual slumber. In the end, the viceroy succeeds in his quest—just as generations of righteous people who maintained their resolve have helped mankind emerge from its spiritual apathy and awaken from its slumber.

In practical terms, this means that eating and sleeping are positive things and we *should* do them. But we have to make sure we use our physical strengths for constructive purposes. Eating is a purification process; it can actually rectify my own sins, as well as sins from previous eras, going back to Adam! I can elevate sparks of holiness merely with a little food and a blessing, and I can revitalize my soul with proper rest and relaxation.

Rebbe Nachman had a follower, R' Dov of Tcherin, who tried to rise early in the morning in order to devote time to serving God. But R' Dov had difficulties staying awake and suffered from headaches. Rebbe Nachman advised him, "Sleep! And eat! Just guard your time!" (*Kokhavey Or*, p. 25).

24

THE ELEMENT OF FIRE

There are luminaries of light, and there are luminaries of fire. One must learn to subjugate the luminaries of fire to the luminaries of light (Likutey Moharan II, 67:1).

REBBE NACHMAN REFERS to the true and righteous leaders as the "luminaries of light," as they bring light and good advice to the people. Opposing them are false and wicked leaders who are called "luminaries of fire," as they burn and eventually cause much damage to everyone and the world at large. The idea of subjugating "fire" to "light" applies equally to ourselves and our character traits. As we examine more of the positive and negative character traits that we have to work with, we note that the element of fire is behind many of them.

● ● ●

HAUGHTINESS OR HUMILITY?

God created so many kinds of people that it's easy to feel haughty sometimes. Everywhere you go, you find people who are less talented, less intelligent, less important and less well-off than you. Beware: Arrogance hurts you more than them. Our Sages state, "Whoever is arrogant, God says, 'I and he cannot dwell in the same world'" (Sotah 4b). Scripture teaches that God dwells within the Jews even if they are impure (see Leviticus 16:16). But when a person is arrogant, God departs from him. Even more than alienating a person from others, arrogance alienates him from God.

Therefore, throughout Rebbe Nachman's writings, we find many advisories and warnings to stay far away from arrogance. It brings poverty (Likutey Moharan I, 4:8), it leads to immorality (ibid., I, 11:3) and to a host of other disasters. Arrogance, thinking of one's own self-importance, creates a shadow that obscures God's light.

On the other hand, the Rebbe teaches that when a person is humble, he can nullify himself before God. His humility diminishes his essence to the point that there is no obstacle to his receiving God's light (ibid., I, 170). Receiving God's light doesn't refer only to sensing His presence. It means receiving the blessings and bounty that God continually sends our way. With his own attitude, an arrogant person creates obstructions to God's presence and His bounty, or to the vessels that receive His blessings.

But what exactly is humility? Is it walking around with a bowed head, reluctant to speak up in a crowd? Many people act humbly in order to impress others, but their humbleness is really self-serving because arrogance motivates their behavior (ibid., I, 11:8).

Rebbe Nachman says that to be humble, you must not belittle yourself. You should know and acknowledge exactly who you are, what you've done, and how much you've accomplished. At the same time, you should honor and respect others as if their being and their accomplishments are all greater than yours (ibid., I, 14:5; II, 72:12). This is not a contradiction. Humility is an attitude that allows you to negate yourself before God. When you think of your insignificance vis-a-vis the Creator, you can adapt a position of insignificance, which then allows you to attain an attitude that others are significant. This does not minimize in any way your true worth, which as a human being is awesome. It just gives you the freedom of adopting the attitude that others are important and we must respect them.

WHAT DOES THIS MEAN TO ME ?

The next time you're upset that things aren't going your way, stop and check what's really happening inside you. The feeling of, "*I* want it this way, and it's not going *my* way," is a sign that the trait of haughtiness has emerged. The way to correct this is to humble yourself and bring God into the equation. Tell God, "I want to do the right thing, but I just can't get my act together." Then God will help you straighten out the things that are going wrong in your life.

• • •

ANGER OR PATIENCE?

Have you ever watched a person get angry? His face turns red, his facial features twist grotesquely, and he looks like he's going to explode. The element of fire destroys his temperament and replaces it with a burning rage. The Kabbalists explain that when a person becomes angry, he not only loses his physical appearance, but he literally tears up his holy soul and replaces it with a soul from the Other Side (of evil), may God spare us (*Zohar* II, 182a; *Sha'ar Ruach HaKodesh*, p. 33).

Anger is representative of Esau, who is called the "great accuser." That is, just as Esau sought to destroy Jacob, so too, anger arouses the accusers on high to mete out punishment for that anger. Furthermore, even on this earth, an angry person is disdained and even despised (see *Likutey Moharan* I, 57:6).

Rebbe Nachman adds that the angry person damages his wealth and possessions. He explains that wealth is a person's *ChoMaH* (חומה), or "wall," which offers him protection. When he gets frustrated and responds with *ChaiMaH* (חמה), "anger," he breaks that wall and opens himself up to damage and loss of his wealth. Patience, on the other hand, is a protective wall, both for one's wisdom and one's wealth. Thus, the Rebbe teaches that every person should be blessed from birth with great wealth, but because of anger that attacks us from infancy, we tend to break down our wall and lose that blessing (ibid., I, 68).

Patience is a very lofty and laudable level. One who attains faith can attain patience, since the two concepts are related. Faith is often referred to as a "growing force" since it helps guide the person on a forward path. As long as a person has faith, he can succeed; he will progress in life towards his goals.

Rebbe Nachman explains the connection between patience and faith with the example of planting seeds in the earth. The soil must be good in order for the seeds to take root and sprout. But even after the seeds take root, one must be patient and wait for them to sprout;

he must wait until the crops ripen before he can harvest them. One who has faith is "planting his seeds" for the future—but he must nourish that faith by exercising patience at every step. This patience allows him to "wait out" all the challenges and frustrations he encounters and eventually succeed (see ibid., I, 155:2).

WHAT DOES THIS MEAN TO ME?

Like haughtiness, anger is a sign that "my wants" and "my needs" override everything else—even God. We usually get mad because our desires aren't fulfilled. By exercising a little patience, we can step away from the heat of the moment and give ourselves some space to reevaluate our goals—and even decide to redirect them—so that our anger can dissipate.

• • •

JEALOUSY OR BENEFICENCE?

Rebbe Nachman taught: The *yetzer hara* (evil inclination or evil characteristics that possess a person) hates man and seeks to harm him, physically and spiritually (*Rabbi Eliyahu Chaim Rosen*).

We can understand that the evil inclination seeks man's spiritual harm, but why his physical harm, too? Just look at how much effort it puts into undermining man's physical and material well-being. The *Zohar* (I, 179a) points out, "Come see the power of the evil inclination. An animal is born with a natural instinct for survival. It senses predators and avoids danger right from birth. Not so the human child. He runs straight towards danger.

He seeks out any perilous situation and jumps right in! This is because he is born with the evil inclination." That inner, burning rage and jealousy, that inborn fire that ignites with passion and turbulence, destroys any chance of inner peace.

One way the evil inclination succeeds in endangering or destroying our physical and emotional well-being is through the trait of jealousy. One of the most ingrained of human attributes, the heat and passion of jealousy emerge at an early age. Even as infants, we desire what someone else has. And, as we all know, it doesn't stop there. Family members, neighbors, colleagues and acquaintances can all be the objects of our envy. Jealousy is arguably the most destructive of traits, because it leaves us without satisfaction or comfort, ever.

Just look at what jealousy has caused: Cain was jealous of his brother Abel so he killed one-quarter of mankind. Joseph's brothers were jealous of him and, as a result, our forefathers went into bondage in Egypt (*Shabbat* 10b). Korach's jealousy of Moses and Aaron (Numbers 16) not only brought about the first rebellion in the history of the Jewish nation, but also caused the deaths of over 14,000 people (ibid., 17:14). King Saul nearly killed King David because of his jealousy towards him. If such outstanding individuals can fall prey to jealousy, what chance do we have? (see *Likutey Moharan* II, 1:1; *Parparaot LeChokhmah*, loc. cit.).

Where does jealousy come from? Rebbe Nachman teaches that jealousy is rooted in the Evil Eye. Often misunderstood as some abstract mystical power, the Evil Eye referred to by the Rebbe is the very commonplace quality of looking at our friends and neighbors in a negative or critical way (see *Likutey Moharan* I, 54:4). The

Talmud describes it as, "someone who is always looking into another's house" (see *Bava Batra* 2b). Rather than thinking positively about our neighbors and friends and wishing them the best, we tend to covet their possessions and their good fortune.

The opposite of jealousy is a beneficial eye. That is, the person always looks kindly and sees the positive side of people. The verse states, "One with a good eye is blessed, for he has given from his bread to the poor" (Proverbs 22:9). When a person takes of his own and extends it to another, he is blessed. The simple meaning is that because he gave from his wealth, he will be blessed by Heaven with additional wealth. But a deeper meaning of the verse is that a person with a benevolent eye is automatically considered "a person who is blessed." Simply put, his good and beneficial eye, giving to others, finding the good in others, having that positive outlook, is itself a phenomenal blessing!

WHAT DOES THIS MEAN TO ME ?

The Talmud speaks of envy as decaying the bones of a deceased person (*Shabbat* 152b). It decays the life of the jealous person, too. Envy brings out so many bad qualities in the jealous person that we should try to avoid it at all costs.

Instead, we can practice beneficence. "Even if you cannot attain a high level yourself, you can still be supportive of others and desire that they attain what you cannot reach," says Rebbe Nachman. "Even if I cannot be a good, religious Jew, at least my friend should be one" (*Rabbi Nachman's Wisdom* #119).

Reb Noson comments: I thought that was obvious. Of course, if I cannot be a good Jew, at least my friend should be one. Of course I wish him success. But as I grew older, I began to realize that this is a major cause of strife and derision among Jews. We see many people who have tried to become truly religious. They exert great effort, make serious attempts, but do not succeed fully and eventually drift away. Instead of encouraging others, they become intolerant and jealous of those who do pray intensely and who do study Torah. "If I can't make it, they also can't (or won't or shouldn't)," they tell themselves—and do whatever they can to prevent others from succeeding. However, a true Jew must do the exact opposite. He should want others to serve God even when he himself is unable to do so. This is true Jewish love! (ibid.).

● ● ●

BRAZENNESS OR BOLDNESS?

Throughout Rebbe Nachman's and Reb Noson's teachings, we find mention of the idea of "being bold." The Hebrew word that appears in their texts is *azut* (עזות). As with many other Hebrew words in general and Rebbe Nachman's often novel use of them in particular, there is no exact translation that incorporates all the connotations that the original, *azut*, carries. Therefore the reader will alternately find in our books either "boldness" or "brazenness." The former is used when the text wishes to convey the positive and desirable quality of *azut*, whereas the latter is used to indicate its negative aspect.

One of the greatest attributes a person can acquire is that of being bold. This means having the gumption to go about his business, or devotions, no matter what the situation. A person should never have to refrain from doing what he wants to do just because others might ridicule him for—or during—his efforts. Still, the *Shulchan Arukh* (*Orach Chaim* 1:1) warns against being brazen, about having chutzpah towards others. The traits of boldness and brazenness both stem from a person's element of fire.

Reb Noson elaborates on these characteristics. First, he explains that boldness parallels faith. One who works on perfecting his faith attains boldness. Conversely, a blemish of faith results in blemished boldness, and the person acquires the negative characteristic of brazenness.

Reb Noson then explains that humility and boldness each have their negative side. Unquestionably, a person must have humility. When someone feels humble and embarrassed before God, he will feel ashamed to ever commit a sin. Yet he must also combine a measure of boldness with his humility. Otherwise, if he is so embarrassed before God, he will never be able to open his mouth to pray to Him—and without prayer, he cannot draw close to God. A person should stand before God in humility either because of God's greatness or due to his own sins. But he must also be bold enough to never hesitate about pleading with God to draw him close and forgive his sins.

The worst type of brazenness is to go against God and commit a sin. But then a different kind of humility—false humility—rears its head. The person begins to feel embarrassed and will refrain from repenting! "After all, I just committed a terrible sin, how can I approach God?" With false humility, a person regresses even more into brazenness. Therefore, Reb Noson says, one always has to weigh his situation very carefully, in order to choose wisely what constitutes holy boldness and humility, and what constitutes brazenness and false humility (*Likutey Halakhot, Halva'ah* 3:3-4).

WHAT DOES THIS MEAN TO ME ?

Although Rebbe Nachman emphasizes the importance of boldness, exactly how, where and when to use it remains undetermined. Indeed, because of the almost infinite number of factors that can come into play in a given situation, it's all but impossible to provide anything more than general principles for using this trait. Therefore the questions that arise concerning the practical application of *azut*, as well as the proper use of humility, can be solved only through prayer. In fact, in his *Likutey Tefilot*, Reb Noson devotes a good portion of the prayers that he composed on the topics in this chapter to pleading with God to be given the proper knowledge to know how, where and when to use each one.

As a simple guide, though, we should always take into consideration that our actions do not cause harm in any way to others, and that we're careful to always speak respectfully to others. That way, whatever we do, we'll succeed in our goals and not be branded as brazen individuals.

• • •

VICTORY OR DEFEAT?

Which would you prefer, victory or defeat? Victory, of course. But what constitutes victory, and how do you define defeat?

Let's face it. Nobody wants to lose an argument. We'll do whatever we can to ensure our success. So we'll argue and present our side and maybe stretch it a little (or a lot) just to prove our point. Along the way, we drop the pretense of seeking the truth and will resort to any and all means to triumph. The same applies when we try to best someone else in business or display our "superiority" over our peers. There's no end to what we'll resort to. But is it really in our best interests?

Rebbe Nachman teaches:

> Our desire to be victorious (*nitzachon* in Hebrew) prevents us from accepting the truth. If, in a conversation or an argument, we recognize the validity of the other person's opinion, we'll pursue our own reasoning rather than accept—or even worse, admit—that the other person may be right (*Likutey Moharan* I, 122).

The character trait of *nitzachon* is a frequently-discussed topic in Reb Noson's writings. He explains that in the Torah, the word for eternal, *NetZaCh* (נצח), also means victory, *NitZaChon* (נצחון). These two meanings are really one. Only that which is eternal can be called a true victory.

History has proved time and again that a conquered nation or an oppressed people will not remain silent forever. It may take years, a new generation may arise, but sooner or later, the cycle of time turns round and the victor—because his victory was not permanent or final—finds himself suffering at the hands of the vanquished. This also holds true on the personal level. "Conquering" one's competitor in business or climbing the social ladder at someone else's expense creates in the loser feelings of hostility and a desire for retribution.

Ultimately, such victories are empty and worthless. For the moment, the person may have achieved his desired goal, but this contributes nothing to his peace of mind for life in this world, or for his eternal life. The real victory, says Reb Noson, is when you conquer your negative characteristics and desires. Then you are the true victor (*Likutey Halakhot, Birkhot Pratiyot* 5:2).

WHAT DOES THIS MEAN TO ME ?

The way to overcome the trait of *nitzachon* is through prayer. Plead with God to help you succeed. Whenever you're faced with a possibility of *nitzachon*, ask God to help you overcome your desire for a victory that is false or temporary at best. Strive only for a *nitzachon* that is eternal. Remember, it's better to lose face (and even more) while saving your eternal soul than resort to conquering others and forcing your way on them.

DAILY
CHALLENGES

EVERY DAY WE FACE choices and temptations in the areas of business and work, speech, thought and morality. Where do these temptations come from? More importantly, what can we do about them?

25

EARNING A LIVING

*It is good when one combines Torah with work; with
the effort placed in both, one can defeat sin* (Avot 2:2).

WHEN GOD CREATED MAN and placed him in the
Garden of Eden, He gave man the opportunity to live
a wonderful life, a healthy life, a spiritual life and a
trouble-free existence. It took but an hour, and Adam
lost everything by eating from the Tree of Knowledge
of Good and Evil. Life spiraled into physical, financial
and emotional chaos, with all of these obscuring man's
spiritual goals.

Adam's eating from the Tree gave rise to three major
physical lusts, known as *ta'avat akhilah* (the desire for
food), *ta'avat mamon* (the desire for wealth and possessions) and *ta'avat mishgal* (the desire for sex). To be sure,
there is no lack of issues that can engulf and overwhelm a
person—the craving for honor or power, health problems,
family stress, and so on—but these three desires in
particular dominate and control each person's time,
effort and concentration. As a direct result of Adam's

transgression, mankind was plunged into an abyss of material wants that became the main focus of life.

Since Adam sinned by *eating* from the Tree, he was subjected to cravings for food and nourishment in order to sustain his body—a lifetime struggle. And to sustain his continuous need for nourishment, Adam was made to work for his livelihood, as it is written, "By the sweat of your brow, you will eat bread" (Genesis 3:19).

Of the three main lusts, the desire for money is the only one that lasts an entire lifetime. For the most part, at certain stages, a person's drive for sensual pleasure wanes and weakens. In old age, a person eats because he requires nourishment; otherwise his appetite is pretty much gone. But the need or desire for money keeps up with him until his dying day.

Money in itself has many positive aspects. The person who has it can readily purchase what he needs. Better yet, he can give to charity, educate his children, spend generously on Shabbat and Jewish festivals, and perform many other *mitzvot*. So having money can be a good thing. However, it's the *burning desire* for money that will keep a person focused on the money itself rather than all the good he can do with it.

For example, there are those who skimp on all their expenses; although they have the means, they don't allow themselves to enjoy life. Then there are those who live beyond their means, cruising through life on plastic cards or someone else's bankroll. There are those who hoard their wealth, those who must have every new gadget, and those who watch their bank accounts and stock portfolios on a daily basis. These are some of the behavioral patterns with which people are individually "blessed." What you have and what you do with it is strictly your own business. What Rebbe Nachman comes to teach us are the reasons for the neurotic fixation on money.

Where does the insatiable desire for money come from? Rebbe Nachman connects it with a lack of knowledge. Since the curse of having to work stems from the sin of eating from the Tree of *Knowledge*, a person who lacks knowledge will want and crave and never be satisfied with his portion (cf. *Avot* 4:1: "Who is wealthy? One who is content with his lot"). This knowledge, or lack of knowledge, which Rebbe Nachman speaks about does not refer to "street smarts" or a broad education. It refers to knowledge of God, of man's purpose in life, of knowing how to live and make the most of every moment. In this context, lack of knowledge means indulging in material desires and possessions (anything a person has a need for is not considered an indulgence).

True, we do see people who are completely lacking in knowledge and yet possess the best of everything. But as the Rebbe says, "In truth, whatever they have is nothing at all." Similarly, if we see a person who does possess perfect knowledge and yet has some lack, we should know that this lack is nothing at all (*Likutey Moharan* I, 21:12).

When it comes to the day-to-day pressures of earning a living, Rebbe Nachman advises that our motivations should not be based on avarice, but on faith. The Talmud explains that each person's annual income is determined in advance by God on Rosh HaShanah (the Jewish New Year) (*Beitzah* 16a). A person who enters the New Year thinking that he has a "guaranteed income" may see his money whittled away by unexpected expenses or doctor bills, while one who barely makes ends meet may receive an unexpected windfall that will bring him up to the amount that God has predetermined for him. In this light, the challenge of earning a living lies not in dealing with the stress of the workplace, but in maintaining our faith that God, and God alone, provides. We must trust in Him to provide us with our needs. With faith, a person can face the difficulties; without faith, he will do anything he can—legally and illegally—to make a buck.

In the dog-eat-dog world of business, it's so tempting to shortchange customers or renege on our word in order to stay ahead. And if no one's aware of our deception, why shouldn't we?

The answer is that the rectification of the world depends on our honesty and integrity in financial matters. Rebbe Nachman explains that just as the desire for eating was a direct result of Adam's sin, so is the desire for money. Adam's sin caused the sparks of holiness to fall into the realm of impurity in all levels of Creation. As a result, sparks of holiness can be found in all minerals, in vegetation and in animal life, as well as in human beings. Business is meant to help elevate these sparks, which is why the Hebrew term for business and trading is *masa u'matan* (משא ומתן), literally, "elevating and giving." Everything that is traded—whether merchandise, raw materials (e.g., textiles, metals or grains), or services rendered to others, like financial services, legal advice and repairs—contains sparks of holiness. As a person works, the sparks are elevated from level to level. Dealing honestly elevates these sparks. Dealing dishonestly can prevent the ascent of the sparks, and even cause them to descend to lower levels.

Each honest deal also builds a Sanctuary. Our Sages explain that Thirty-Nine Types of Labor were required to build the Sanctuary in the desert (*Bava Kama* 2a). Rebbe Nachman teaches that one who works honestly and with faith finds that his efforts are sanctified, and thus his work can be considered as building a Sanctuary. In contrast, one who lacks faith will find that all he does is *work*. He may be an inventor or a famous researcher who discovers new things, but because his efforts do not create anything directly associated with an enhanced knowledge of God, they are futile. Such work is solely the result of the curse of Adam. A person who has faith not only helps rectify the curse placed on Adam, but he also merits to draw blessing into his life and into the world at large.

WHAT DOES THIS MEAN TO ME ?

Work. One way or another, we all have to do it. As the Midrash teaches, "God created man in a manner that he is like an indentured slave for life: if he doesn't work, he doesn't eat" (*Bereishit Rabbah* 14:10).

In a simple sense, man must eat to sustain his body. If he nourishes his body, he can live; without nourishment, he can't. But the Midrash is actually a commentary on what Rebbe Nachman calls "knowledge." That is, if a person works to acquire knowledge of God, then he will always have what to "eat" in the World to Come.

Of course, in this world, we do need to earn a living and support our families. But to what degree? Am I supposed to spend all of my life in material pursuit? Or should I pursue a career in a field where I am better able to manage my life and set aside time for myself, my family and my spiritual devotions?

Rebbe Nachman was well aware of the necessity to engage in a livelihood, a topic discussed in many of his lessons. He was even more aware of the pressing demands of time placed on the person who wishes to flee the indentured servitude of work for a life of spiritual attainments. A perfect balance between the two is difficult to maintain. But one who is indentured to wealth will find that throughout his whole life, he is mortgaged to his needs and possessions. Someone who seeks a spiritual life will find respite and even rest from the daily grind. Witness the freedom of Shabbat. Even someone who must spend full days building his business or working for others has at least one spiritual day of rest a week where he can experience freedom from his servitude.

26

SPEECH

IN CHAPTER 22 we saw that four elements influence the human character. Fire corresponds to arrogance and anger, water is the source of the pleasures a person seeks, and earth is the root of laziness and depression. All humans have these traits, as well as all animals.

The one trait that distinguishes man from animal is the power of speech, which corresponds to the element of air. Air is the root of our words—these words are breathed out from our bodies and then "travel" on the air waves until they reach the person they're addressed to. Air also refers to the tendency to speak worthless subjects and forbidden speech such as flattery, profanity, falsehood, slander, mockery, and the like. Air—speech—is also the source of boasting.

Speech takes a place of major importance in Rebbe Nachman's writings. The Rebbe teaches, "Not all speech can be considered as words," as it states in Psalms, "It is not speech, it is not words, if they are not heard" (Psalms 19:4). The Rebbe explains that the reason one's words are not heard is because they lack good—they lack knowledge and awareness of good (*Likutey Moharan* I, 29:1).

We all know what kind of speech Rebbe Nachman is talking about. Gossip, backbiting, flattery, profanity and slander have become socially acceptable in modern society. Gossip and idle words are very tempting to listen to; as the adage goes, "Make sure you're at the party you're invited to—otherwise you'll be the subject of the conversation!" Gossip draws people's attention, but in the end, "it is not speech, it is not words," for it goes nowhere towards building our lives. On the contrary—it destroys relationships and ruins reputations. Rebbe Nachman compares forbidden speech to a hurricane. It doesn't last, but the devastation left in its wake takes months or years to overcome—if at all.

Words are more than just a means of communicating our ideas. Words express our feelings, channel our energies, and transport our inner beings to where we want to be. Words have tremendous power. They can penetrate another's heart, whether we're speaking sincerely to family and friends, petitioning the boss for a raise, or entreating a policeman who's about to write a speeding ticket to let us off the hook. Words can even go beyond our physical sphere to convey our desires directly to God. Through our words of prayer, we create a vessel that allows us to send and receive messages, which translates as sending and receiving blessing!

Rebbe Nachman says that when a person speaks in the proper manner, his speech can permeate the air around him and positively influence those who are distant from God—even those who don't live in his vicinity (ibid., I, 17:5; I, 62:4).

The Rebbe also teaches that proper speech can break down the walls that prevent you from reaching your goals. All you need to do is learn how to articulate your speech before God, which can be done during *hitbodedut* (private prayer) or at any time of day. Say it! Say it with fervor! Say it with love for God or fear of Him! But say it! Say to God, "I want this, I want that." By articulating your thoughts before God, you build your desire for good until you attain the goals you seek (see ibid., I, 66:4).

The power of positive and encouraging speech is absolutely incredible. At the same time, the destructive force of forbidden speech is unbelievably devastating. Rebbe Nachman calls the latter type of speech, "the end of all flesh" (Genesis 6:13), since it results in the destruction of the people it talks about, as well as those who hear and absorb its evil. An example would be the media, which rarely has a good word to say about anybody. Don't you feel uptight and concerned, actually very worried and nervous, every time they conclude the evening news, all because of what they deemed important to tell you? Didn't anything good happen during the day or week? Therefore Rebbe Nachman emphasizes the importance of good and positive speech. Imagine how much joy would fill the world if we all spoke only good and kind words!

WHAT DOES THIS MEAN TO ME ?

In today's world of emails and texting, the art of communication has been lost. Once upon a time, people used to spend time composing their thoughts, and writing and rewriting letters to make sure the receiver would understand exactly what they wanted to say. Today people zip off text messages faster than they can even think the words, and the potential for misunderstanding and hurt are rife.

The *Zohar* compares speech to the *sefirah* of *Malkhut* (Kingship) (*Tikkuney Zohar* 17a). On a simple level, this means that speech is the means of authority, and the way in which a person can be viewed. Use your speech wisely and sparingly, and people will view you as sensitive and caring. Use wrongful speech, and you'll be viewed as inelegant and crude. Use kind and positive speech, and people will listen to you; you have, after all, a way of conveying good that everyone seeks.

Rebbe Nachman is an ardent supporter of always looking for and finding the good in others and in ourselves (see Chapter 11, "What are the Good Points?"). One of the major ways to achieve this is by speaking clean, caring and meaningful words. When you think good, you'll speak good. After all, you do have mastery over your words.

27

THE IMAGINATION

Today we have to call the evil inclination by a new name: the imagination (*Likutey Moharan* I, 25:9).

THE HUMAN BRAIN IS an incredible, computer-like machine that processes millions upon millions of bits of information each day. Everything we see, hear, touch, taste and feel goes into our brains. Our memories of past events do not disappear, but remain stored in our minds and influence our future decision-making. This is one reason why we should steer clear of temptations that appear before us, lest they cloud our judgment.

There also exists another stimulus for the brain. This is a person's imagination. The information absorbed in the brain remains in the recesses of the memory. At times, even a single word or sight can trigger that information, which then ignites the person's passions. Worse, a person can intentionally "enter" into the realm of creative thought and remain fixated on his ideas. This can be extremely beneficial if the person seeks quality and goodness. But it could also be exceedingly destructive. It all depends on your focus.

In the 21st century, the imagination is running amok. What people can dream up today is absolutely incredible: thanks to computer graphics, computer-generated imagery and virtual worlds, a person can conjure up real and unreal images at the click of a mouse. The depravity engendered by the internet and violent video games knows no bounds, as we see from the proliferation of crime and even murder inspired by virtual fantasies. Rebbe Nachman summed it up succinctly when he observed, "You are where your thoughts are" (*Likutey Moharan* I, 21:12). His Chassidim took this a step further and added, "Make sure your thoughts are where you want to be."

In our discussion of the four elements (see Chapter 22), we noted that the element of water brings enjoyment to the entire world, to all levels of mineral, vegetable, animal and human. Therefore water is the root of all sensual gratification. Reb Noson once said that at its root, water is extremely lofty, since it was one of the first things to be created and from it, most other things were created. Therefore it brings great pleasure and enjoyment to mankind (*Sichot v'Sippurim* #2, p. 69). We can also apply the idea of sensual pleasure to man's imagination. It can bring him great comfort and pleasure when he imagines his goals being attained, and other similar rewards. But this same pleasure can easily become man's obsession. It can engulf his mind and body with thoughts and urges that prevent him from focusing on worthwhile goals.

Is it really possible to control our thoughts? Rebbe Nachman assures us that it is. He compares thought to a wayward horse that has turned away from the path and is trying to head off in the wrong direction. The rider need only pull on the bridle to force the horse back onto the path. In the same way, a person's thoughts are completely under his control (*Likutey Moharan* II, 50).

Of course it's not simple. Everything around us stimulates the mind, and our memories combined with our imagination can easily distract us. Is there any hope? Yes. Rebbe Nachman advises that the best way to deal with unwanted thoughts is simply to ignore them. "Act as if you were completely unconcerned. Refuse to listen. Carry on with what you are doing—studying, praying, working, and so on. Pay no attention to the thoughts or fantasies at all. Don't keep looking around to see if they have gone away. Just carry on with what you are trying to do. In the end, they will go away of their own accord" (ibid., I, 72).

Thought-control doesn't happen overnight. But when we exercise self-control as often as possible, we learn that we *can* do it. We need only pull on the reins to stop and redirect our thoughts, and then *we* control our imaginations, not the other way around.

WHAT DOES THIS MEAN TO ME ?

Your mind is a wondrous machine with amazing potential: the *Zohar* teaches that one who works on controlling his thoughts actually makes his head a sanctuary for God! (see *Tikkuney Zohar* #21, p. 63a). But there are battles to overcome to attain a pure mind. Rebbe Nachman compares the battle of the mind to the ancient coliseums where kings would pit one creature against another. According to the *Zohar*, the "creatures" are the angels that carry God's Chariot, as it were (see Ezekiel 1). The forces of impurity represent the impure creatures that bring evil thoughts to mind. When a person directs his mind to good, he overpowers the evil creatures and invokes the power of the good and kind angels (*Likutey Moharan* I, 233). Yes, a person has that power within himself.

You can also use to your advantage the fact that the mind cannot hold two thoughts at the same time. No matter what you're thinking about, the minute you introduce a new thought, the previous thought gets relegated to the background and disappears automatically. Try it for yourself. If you're listening to a sports game and suddenly someone bursts into the room to tell you an exciting piece of news, you won't be able to concentrate on both things at once. Even in the midst of an important business matter, an interruption diverts the mind to the new area. Any thought can dislodge another—including thoughts about God, Torah, and even work and daily interests (ibid.).

We can't always stop thoughts and fantasies from entering our minds. But we do have the power to reject them once we become conscious of them. And this is how we can make amends for the mistakes we may have committed earlier in our lives, when we weren't so careful about what we chose to think about. As Rebbe Nachman puts it, "Perfect repentance has to balance the original sins exactly, and this is literally what happens here. Before, when he sinned, it was because the temptation entered his mind and he succumbed to it. Now the thought is in his mind again, but this time he rejects it" (cf. ibid., I, 26). In a flash, a person can turn the tables on the intrusive evil thoughts that plague him and seize control of his mind!

So don't feel discouraged if you find all kinds of temptations and fantasies continually bombarding your thoughts. They are actually providing you with the opportunity to repent and make amends for the damage done in the past. *Today* you have the power to master your thoughts and temptations. When you do so, the sparks of holiness that shattered and fell because of your earlier transgressions are released and you are able to purify yourself. Your mind and your voice will be purified and you will find harmony and peace. This peace can bring the whole world back to the service of God.

28

THE MORAL DILEMMA

The main evil inclination is in sexual matters (*Likutey Moharan* I, 2:9).

ADAM'S SIN OF EATING from the Tree of Knowledge gave rise to three major physical lusts that would affect all future generations: *ta'avat akhilah* (the desire for food), *ta'avat mamon* (the desire for money) and *ta'avat mishgal* (the desire for sex). We can understand the desire for food as stemming from the sin of *eating* from the Tree, and the desire for money as being an extension of the need to acquire and work for that food. But where does the desire for sex fit in to his act?

The ARI explains that a lesser-known aspect of Adam's sin was the element of sexual lust. The phrase "eating from the Tree of Knowledge" is a euphemism implying that Adam and Eve cohabitated on the Friday they were created, before the onset of Shabbat (*Pri Etz Chaim, Sha'ar Rosh HaShanah* 4, p. 557). The Tree is called the *Etz HaDa'at* (עץ הדעת), "Tree of Knowledge," with the word "knowledge" implying a union, as in, "And Adam *knew* his wife" (Genesis 4:1). Adam and Eve acted impulsively, not waiting to unite on Shabbat, when marital relations are encouraged and indeed heighten the sanctity of the day (*Ketuvot* 62b; *Orach Chaim* 280:1). Thus, they implanted in all of humankind the immoral thoughts and lustful urges that we all experience.

Rebbe Nachman teaches that the most consuming desire is the sexual drive, and he often quotes the *Zohar* (III, 15b): "The main evil inclination is for sexual promiscuity, which is the fundamental source of defilement."

Reb Noson writes that the Rebbe ridiculed the obsessive sexual drive, quoting the words of the morning prayers: "Do not bring me to a test or to disgrace." The Rebbe said, "Either a test, or else disgrace." That is, if you do not pass the test, you will come to disgrace (*Rabbi Nachman's Wisdom* #304).

We have become so desensitized by our contemporary, "anything goes" society that the idea of disgrace never enters our minds. Rebbe Nachman may have lived in the 19th century, but his vision was very much focused on 21st-century man. He immediately followed that last statement with this comment: "People are so bound up with their bodily desires, and tied to this one in particular, that it does not help when you explain how base this is. On the contrary, the more you speak of it, the more lewd thoughts they have. Therefore, in most cases, it is best not to even begin to think of it at all" (ibid.).

Marriage is a mitzvah—actually, it's the very first mitzvah the Torah commands—so there are very positive aspects to the innate physical desire to procreate. To perform this mitzvah, a person becomes focused on earning a living to support his family, he understands the importance of setting moral parameters for his family, and he realizes the significance of living honestly in order to pass on that legacy to his children. Many great things come from this approach to a union between husband and wife.

But when removed from the sanctity of marriage, the sexual desire leads to all sorts of immoral behavior. Lewd thoughts can pervade a person's mind and literally occupy it for days on end. Extramarital affairs are dishonesty at its worst, and the necessary cover-ups entangle the person in a web of lies and deceit that only gets worse over time. For those who seek a relationship without commitment, the arrangement ends in broken promises anyway. Witness those who live with each other for five years to see if it "works." After they marry, they divorce within a year or two, wondering why, if they "tried" it for so many years, it didn't work. Homosexuality is unnatural, even for those who claim it is natural to them, for people were not designed to unite in that manner. It just doesn't work.

Perhaps worst of all is the sin of masturbation. Far from being a spur of the moment lapse, immorality has repercussions that extend throughout the length and breadth of creation. The Talmud teaches that because of his sin, Adam became subjected to temptation, and for a period of 130 years he committed masturbation, the abusive sin of wasting seed (*Eruvin* 18b). This sin, in turn, caused the exile in Egypt and the decree of all subsequent exiles. The reason is that each drop of semen contains life—souls and sparks of holiness. When this seed is wasted, God forbid, it becomes a "soul without a body." Ungrounded, it is then cast about and spread all over the world. The only way to rectify such a sin is to go about collecting all those sparks that were cast all over. Exile serves the purpose of retrieving the sparks and gathering them in to be rectified (see *Sha'ar HaPesukim, Shemot; Likutey Moharan* II, 92).

Since Adam's time, the very great Tzaddikim have been working hard to find a rectification for the sin of immorality, as we find in the holy writings. Rebbe Nachman himself revealed the *Tikkun HaKlali* (General Remedy), which is a spiritual rectification for wasted seed in particular and all other kinds of sins in general. The *Tikkun HaKlali* consists of ten Psalms, recited in this order: 16, 32, 41, 42, 59, 77, 90, 105, 137, 150 (see *Likutey Moharan* II, 92). Both men and women can say the *Tikkun HaKlali* daily and thereby effect rectification for sexual sin.

WHAT DOES THIS MEAN TO ME ?

So, what are we to do about the desire for sex? Even more, what *can* we do about it? The Torah permits pleasure and encourages a person to bear children, so sexual relations cannot be a sinful act. The problem is when we take it out of the realm of marriage and spin fantasies in our minds.

As always, Rebbe Nachman approaches the problem straightforwardly. There are things that are permitted and there are things that are forbidden. And there are temptations that crop up and can lead the person onto an immoral path and way of life. Our goal in any situation must be to guard the covenant (see Chapter 15, "What is the Covenant?"). We can fortify our resolve by remembering the far-reaching spiritual repercussions of immorality, not to mention the physical, emotional and financial devastation caused by wasted seed. This is because seed is life-bearing and, as such, is a blessing. Blessing can be found in having children, in emotional stability, in good health and in financial success. We can achieve these if we strive to live a clean and pure life.

The guarded covenant is known as *BOAZ* (בועז), a word that incorporates the Hebrew words *BO AZ* (בו עז), "in him is strength." Someone who does what he can to live morally is considered a man of great strength. The Mishnah concurs, "Who is mighty? He who conquers his inclination" (*Avot* 4:1).

Rebbe Nachman teaches that living morally yields great rewards. Guarding one's covenant brings a person an easy livelihood (*Likutey Moharan* I, 29:5). One who is morally directed can also find the correct counsel that he needs, since a pure mind is able to filter out the "chaff from the wheat" (the clogged remnants of the brain as opposed to the purer parts that can guide him correctly) (cf. ibid., I, 7:4). Morality protects a person from arrogance and many other evil character traits (see ibid., I, 11:3). Honest relationships help a person pray better; after all, he is not trying to hide his iniquities while asking for his heart's desires (ibid., I, 2:2). A purer mind can better absorb Torah teachings (cf. ibid., I, 19:6-8; I, 27:4-6; I, 101). And morality brings peace (ibid., I, 27:6).

In short, there is no limit to the good—health, financial, emotional and, of course, spiritual attainments—that can be attained when a person leads a moral life. The converse is also true. So which will it be? What do we aim for? The Kabbalists teach that guarding the covenant and living morally parallels the *sefirah* of *Yesod*. Yesod translates as "Foundation." Living morally is the best and strongest foundation anyone can have in life.

REBBE NACHMAN IS
ALL ABOUT YOU

IN THIS BOOK we have outlined the most basic ideas presented in Rebbe Nachman's teachings. Of course there's more. Lots more. But these are the focal points of the Rebbe's writings to help you draw close to God. And to yourself—which is the only way you can truly draw close to God.

This is because Rebbe Nachman is really about you. His teachings are meant to help you get in touch with yourself, define your strengths and weaknesses, and learn to live a simpler life so you can make the most of each day.

Rebbe Nachman's teachings get right to the point. They focus on the here and now, on the task at hand. They talk about what a person can feel and the abilities he possesses—not what is beyond his capabilities or out of his reach. The Rebbe encourages you to use your own individual strengths, not something someone else has managed. You are your own self—a beautiful, wonderful, incredible human being with your own resources. Use them!

And always remember, you are God's child. You are His favorite child. You are His only and favorite child. So turn to Him. Make Him part of your life. Incorporate Him into your daily routine. Then you will be able to live each moment as it comes and exult in a new life of simplicity and goodness, as you merit making the best of what life presents to you.

After all, it's all about you.

GUIDE TO FURTHER STUDY

To learn more about Rebbe Nachman and Breslov Chasidut, we recommend the following introductory works published by the Breslov Research Institute:

INTRODUCTION TO BRESLOV

Crossing the Narrow Bridge:
A Practical Guide to Rebbe Nachman's Teachings

7 Pillars of Faith and A Day in the Life of a Breslover Chassid

●

PRAYER AND CHASSIDIC MEDITATION

Where Earth and Heaven Kiss:
A Guide to Rebbe Nachman's Path of Meditation

The Sweetest Hour:
Tikkun Chatzot

Entering the Light:
Prayers to Experience the Joy & Wonder
of Shabbat and Yom Tov

Between me & You:
Heartfelt Prayers for Each Jewish Woman

●

KABBALAH

Anatomy of the Soul

Hidden Treasures:
How to Realize Your Potential

•

REBBE NACHMAN'S TEACHINGS

Likutey Moharan (15 vol.)

Rabbi Nachman's Stories

The Aleph-Bet Book

Rabbi Nachman's Wisdom

Rabbi Nachman's Tikkun

•

BRESLOV BIOGRAPHIES

Tzaddik:
A Portrait of Rabbi Nachman

Until the Mashiach:
The Life of Rabbi Nachman

Through Fire and Water:
The Life of Reb Noson of Breslov

•

UMAN

Uman! Uman! Rosh HaShanah!:
A Guide for Travelers to Rebbe Nachman's
Rosh HaShanah Gathering in Uman

Rebbe Nachman and the Knights of the Rosh HaShanah Table:
The Modern-Day Adventures of People Who Found
Their Way to Uman

The Breslov Research Institute also produces music CDs featuring the authentic melodies of Breslov Chassidut.

For a free catalog, email us at info@breslov.org, phone us (in North America) at 1-800-33-BRESLOV (1-800-33-273-7568), or visit our website at www.breslov.org/bookstore.

THE ORDER OF THE TEN SEFIROT

כתר
KETER
|
חכמה
CHOKHMAH
|
בינה
BINAH
|
⎡ דעת ⎤
⎣ DA'AT ⎦
|
חסד
CHESED
|
גבורה
GEVURAH
|
תפארת
TIFERET
|
נצח
NETZACH
|
הוד
HOD
|
יסוד
YESOD
|
מלכות
MALKHUT

THE STRUCTURE OF THE SEFIROT

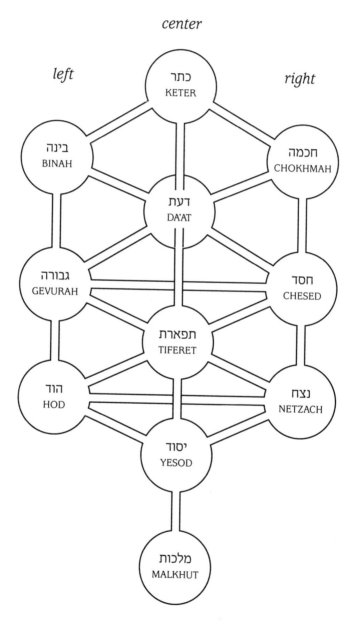

center

left

right

כתר
KETER

בינה
BINAH

חכמה
CHOKHMAH

דעת
DA'AT

גבורה
GEVURAH

חסד
CHESED

תפארת
TIFERET

הוד
HOD

נצח
NETZACH

יסוד
YESOD

מלכות
MALKHUT

HEBREW / ENGLISH TRANSLITERATION SCHEMA

lamed	L	ל	*aleph*	silent*	א
mem	M	מ, ם	*bet*	B	בּ
nun	N	נ, ן	*vet*	V	ב
samekh	S	ס	*gimel*	G	ג
ayin	silent*	ע	*dalet*	D	ד
pei	P	פּ	*hei*	H	ה
phei	Ph, F	פ, ף	*vav*	V, O, U	ו, וֹ, וּ
tzadi	tZ	צ, ץ	*zayin*	Z	ז
kuf	K	ק	*chet*	Ch	ח
reish	R	ר	*tet*	T	ט
shin	Sh	שׁ	*yod*	Y	י
sin	S	שׂ	*kaf*	K	כּ
tav	T	ת	*khaf*	Kh	כ, ך

* The letters א and ע are "silent" consonants (with no English letter-equivalents) and are transliterated based on their accompanying vowel-point as A (Æ), E, I, O (Œ), or U.

HEBREW LETTER NUMEROLOGY (GEMATRIA)

300 = שׁ	70 = ע	20 = כ,ך	6 = ו	1 = א
400 = ת	80 = פ,ף	30 = ל	7 = ז	2 = ב
	90 = צ,ץ	40 = מ,ם	8 = ח	3 = ג
	100 = ק	50 = נ,ן	9 = ט	4 = ד
	200 = ר	60 = ס	10 = י	5 = ה

Alternate values for the 5 end-letters, *MaNtZPaKh*:

900 = ץ	800 = ף	700 = ן	600 = ם	500 = ך

GLOSSARY

ARI: acronym for Rabbi Yitzchak Luria (1534-1572), Jewish scholar and founder of the modern study of Kabbalah

BAAL SHEM TOV: Master of the Good Name, the appellation for Rabbi Yisrael ben Eliezer (1700-1760), founder of Chassidut and great-grandfather of Rebbe Nachman of Breslov

BRIT MILAH: covenant of circumcision

CHANUKAH: eight-day festival commemorating the rededication of the Holy Temple following the victory of the Maccabees over the Greek Empire

CHASSID (pl. CHASSIDIM): a member of a Chassidic group (see *Chassidut*)

CHASSIDUT: a Jewish revival movement founded in Eastern Europe in the 18th century by Rabbi Yisrael ben Eliezer, the Baal Shem Tov. One of its core teachings is that God's presence fills all one's surroundings, and one should strive to serve God in every word and deed.

GEHINNOM: Hell

HALAKHAH: Jewish law

HITBODEDUT: a form of private, secluded prayer and verbal meditation. Rebbe Nachman uses the term to refer to a daily practice in which one sets aside a time and place to speak to God.

KABBALAH: body of mystical Jewish wisdom

KIBUTZ: gathering, especially the annual Rosh HaShanah gathering of Breslover Chassidim by Rebbe Nachman's grave in Uman

LULAV: one of the Four Species that are taken together and waved in all directions during the holiday of Sukkot

MALKHUT: kingship; when capitalized, refers to the lowest of the Ten Sefirot

MATZAH: unleavened bread eaten on Pesach

MIDRASH (pl. MIDRASHIM): homiletical Rabbinic teachings

MINYAN: quorum of at least ten men required for a communal prayer service

MISHNAH: the redaction of the Oral Law which forms the first part of the Talmud, redacted in the second century C.E.

MITZVAH (pl. MITZVOT): Torah commandment or precept

PESACH: the Jewish Passover, a biblical festival commemorating the Exodus from Egypt

PURIM: holiday commemorating the salvation of the Jewish people after they were threatened by a royal edict in ancient Persia

RAV: rabbi, teacher

RASHI: acronym for Rabbi Shlomo Yitzchaki (1040-1110), the preeminent commentator on the Talmud and Tanakh whose commentary appears in all standard editions of these works

ROSH HASHANAH: the Jewish New Year

ROSH YESHIVAH: dean of a Talmudic academy

SEFIRAH (pl. SEFIROT): one of the ten Divine emanations through which all entities on all levels of creation came into being and are continually recreated *ex nihilo*. These emanations are: Keter, Chokhmah, Binah, [Da'at,] Chesed, Gevurah, Tiferet, Netzach, Hod, Yesod and Malkhut.

SHABBAT: the Jewish Sabbath, beginning at sundown on Friday afternoon and ending on Saturday night with the appearance of three medium-sized stars in the night sky

SHEMA: a declaration of faith in the Oneness of God and a commitment to fulfilling His commandments, comprised of verses from Deuteronomy 6:4-9 and 11:13-21 and Numbers 15:37-41. Recited daily during morning and evening prayers, and before going to sleep.

SHOFAR: ram's horn, traditionally blown during Rosh HaShanah morning prayer services

SHULCHAN ARUKH: Code of Jewish Law, compiled by Rabbi Yosef Caro (1488-1575), the benchmark of *halakhah* for all Jews

SIDDUR: Jewish prayer book

SUKKAH: a thatch-covered structure of three or four walls used as a residence during the festival of Sukkot

SUKKOT: biblical festival commemorating God's benevolent care of the Jewish people during their forty-year sojourn in the desert, and His continuing Providence over material blessing

TALMUD: the Jewish Oral Law, expounded by the rabbinical leaders between approximately 50 B.C.E. and 500 C.E. The first part of the Talmud, called the Mishnah, was codified by Rabbi Yehudah HaNasi around 188 C.E. The second part, called the Gemara, was edited by Rav Ashi and Ravina around 505 C.E.

TANAKH: acronym for *Torah, Nevi'im, Ketuvim* (Torah, Prophets, Writings), comprising the twenty-four books of the Hebrew Bible

TEFILIN: mitzvah of wearing special leather boxes on the head and the arm during morning prayers (except on Shabbat and Jewish festivals); the boxes themselves, which contain biblical verses declaring the Oneness of God and the miracles of the Exodus from Egypt

TIKKUN (pl.TIKKUNIM): repair, correction, refinement, perfection, spiritual rectification

TIKKUN HAKLALI: Rebbe Nachman's "General Remedy," the recital of ten specific Psalms that rectify sins (especially sexual transgressions) at their root

TORAH: the Written Law given by God to Moses on Mount Sinai

TZADDIK (pl. TZADDIKIM): a righteous person; in Chassidic thought, one who has purified his heart of all evil, making himself a channel for Divine revelation and true compassion

TZITZIT: specially spun and tied strings which Jewish men are required to affix to their four-cornered garments, as stipulated in Numbers 15:37-41 and discussed in *Menachot* 43b

YESOD: foundation; when capitalized, refers to one of the Ten Sefirot

YHVH: the ineffable four-letter Name of God, also known as the Tetragrammaton

YOM KIPPUR: the Day of Atonement, on which Jewish males age thirteen and over and Jewish females age twelve and over are required to fast from sundown until the appearance of three medium-sized stars the following night

ZOHAR: the greatest classic of Kabbalah, a mystical commentary on the Torah authored by the school of Rabbi Shimon bar Yochai, a Mishnaic Sage and leading disciple of Rabbi Akiva, during the second century C.E.